THE BIBLE DEVOTIONAL

VOLUME I | BOOK BY BOOK
FROM GENESIS TO REVELATION

EDWARD GOBLE

For more information contact:
Ed Goble
edgoble.com

ISBN—13: 9781686180033

Design Concept and Typography—Patrick Pollei
Cover photo © Iakov Kalinin—licensed through 1223RF.com
Back cover photo © Danece Adams for DaneceAdamsPhotography.com

The book is dedicated to my dear wife and the love of my life, MaryAnn.

Acknowledgments

Special thanks to MaryAnn who went through each of these words carefully and prayerfully as my help-mate and confidant., writing down each prayer as a reminder of the goodness and priority of our Lord in this work. We both believe that taking it upon oneself to write about God's Holy Word is not something to be entered into without due consideration as it is to each of these words we will ultimately be held to account. Lord have mercy.

Thanks to our dear children, Kelly, Danece and Melissa, each one contributing from their abundant spiritual gifts to this effort. Their lives reflect both the joy of the Lord and the Hope of the world.

To my editors; MaryAnn Goble, Melissa Johnson, Joan McKinney, and Debbie Jenkins Cook, thank you for your expertise and guidance. Please note, I did not apply all of the advice so kindly given, probably to my embarrasement, so I can state rather confidently that any lingering errors in the manuscript are mine and mine alone.

To George Gates who has been encouraging and prodding me to finish this book for over a decade, thank you my dear friend.

To our friends and dear ones far and wide—Let the word of Christ dwell in you richly in all wisdom, teaching and admonishing one another in psalms and hymns and spiritual songs, singing with grace in your hearts to the Lord. Colossians 3:16 NKJV

CONTENTS

INTRODUCTION

the
Bible
devotional

The Bible. It is the most beautiful, timeless, revered book in recorded history. It is the story of God and the story of man. It is the Word of God, the Breath of the Spirit and the unveiling, in space and time, of God the Son, Jesus Christ; Lord, Messiah, Savior and King.

Paupers, princes and kings stand in awe at its wisdom, fall prostrate before its power and discover its loving, eternal author, to be holy, omnipotent, gentle and kind.

The Bible is one book containing many books. There are sixty-six individual books between the covers of the Bible, bound together by the scarlet thread of redemption that weaves, from Genesis to Revelation, a tapestry of God's plan for mankind and the revelation of the Savior of the world. It is at the same time ancient and timeless, universal and personal. It is God's message to mankind, past, present and future, and God's personal, intimate communication with you.

Jesus, the Christ, the central person and focus of the Bible, is revealed in person closer to the end than the beginning, though He is referred to in symbol or prophecy on nearly every page. His earthly life is chronicled in the Gospels of Matthew, Mark, Luke and John in the beginning of the New Testament.

Emmanuel, God with us, born in a manger in Bethlehem and culminating on the cross of Calvary where Jesus took upon Himself the sins of the world, past, present and future and died for you and me. In three days, He rose from the grave, came back to life bodily, literally shed the garments that bound Him and walked away from the burial tomb alive, eating, serving and talking with over 500 people for forty days before He ascended, alive, into heavenly realms before the eyes of the watching disciples.

INTRODUCTION

Through His sacrificial death, burial and resurrection Jesus defeated death, hell and the grave for all humankind, once and for all, making Him the rightful Lord and King of all ages. The Bible is His story.

This book, The Bible Devotional, is written to be a companion to your personal devotions, a simple reminder that God has spoken, and is speaking, to mankind through the action, drama, poetry, sadness, victory, prophecy and praise of the Bible.

My hope is that this little book stirs a hunger in your soul to open your Bible and read it more reverently and expectantly than ever before, listening for God's loving, affirming voice in your life.

God be with you, dear one.
Edward Goble
July 2019

- - - *The Book Of* - - -

GENESIS

we
all
need

the *Pentateuch*

The first five books of the Bible comprise what are referred to as "The Books of the Law" or the Pentateuch, which is a big, ancient-sounding word that means "Five Books."

Genesis, the first book of the law, is known as the book of beginnings, which is what the word Genesis means, beginnings or origin, that moment when something came into existence, which in this case is everything. We don't know exactly how God did it, although the Apostle John, in the New Testament, is given insight by the Holy Spirit that God the Son— Jesus, whom John refers to as the Word, was present in the beginning, and that everything came into existence through Him.

> In the beginning the Word already existed. The Word was with God, and the Word was God. He existed in the beginning with God. God created everything through him, and nothing was created except through him. The Word gave life to everything that was created, and his life brought light to everyone. John 1:1-4 NLT

While in Genesis, Moses sums up the creation story with the most profound understatement in all of literature:

> In the beginning, God created the heaven and the earth. Genesis 1:1 KJV

Genesis recounts creation and the first humans whose selfish choices led to exile from the paradise God had made for them.

> So the Lord God banished them from the Garden of Eden, and

> he sent Adam out to cultivate the ground from which he had been
> made. Genesis 3:23 NLT

Genesis reveals the emergence of Satan, portrayed in the narrative as a serpent, the great deceiver, who would forever antagonize God's creation. Prophetically, Moses is inspired to write of a future day when the "seed of the woman," the Messiah, would once and for all crush the head of the serpent, even as the serpent would nip at the Messiah's heel.

> And I will put enmity between thee and the woman, and between
> thy seed and her seed; it shall bruise thy head, and thou shalt bruise
> his heel. Genesis 3:15 KJV

In addition to Adam and Eve, the main character in the first chapters of Genesis is Noah, the great servant of God who found grace in God's eyes at a time when the world had become corrupt and evil.

> The Lord observed the extent of human wickedness on the
> earth, and he saw that everything they thought or imagined was
> consistently and totally evil. So the Lord was sorry he had ever
> made them and put them on the earth. It broke his heart. And
> the Lord said, "I will wipe this human race I have created from the
> face of the earth. Yes, and I will destroy every living thing—all the
> people, the large animals, the small animals that scurry along the
> ground, and even the birds of the sky. I am sorry I ever made them."
> But Noah found favor with the Lord. Genesis 6:5-8 NLT

God delivered Noah and his family, along with representatives of the rest of His creation, on a homemade boat through a great flood that destroyed the rest of the flesh on earth.

The rest of Genesis, beginning in chapter 12, follows the family of Abraham, among whom a running theme, that had been hinted at with Adam, Eve and Noah, becomes clear...

Humans have needs

Humans were never intended to exist outside of relationship with other people or, especially, without their Creator. Pride might try and convince us that we don't need anyone or anything, but that's not how God formed us.

We need others and we need God.

Need is both an underlying theme of Genesis and a running trait of mankind. As self-sufficient as we may think we are, there are some things we still need. It's not a bad thing, if we know where to look for help which, in these stories, the characters usually did. Historically, our main problem has been looking for help in all the wrong places.

Adam and Eve needed a covering after they sinned, and God provided.

> **Unto Adam also and to his wife did the Lord God make coats of skins, and clothed them. Genesis 3:21 KJV**

Noah needed a foreman for the boat job, and God provided guidance.

> **Thus did Noah; according to all that God commanded him, so did he. Genesis 6:22 KJV**

The same was true of Abraham and his descendants. Abraham needed a provider, and He trusted that God would be that provision. He told his son Isaac on the way up Mt. Moriah, "God will provide Himself a lamb," and He did.

> **And Abraham said, My son, God will provide himself a lamb for a**

burnt offering: so they went both of them together. Genesis 22:8 KJV
Just before Abraham brought down the knife to sacrifice his son as God had told him, God stopped him and provided the animal. Abraham even named the place, "The Lord Will Provide. "

Note the beautiful, prophetic way that Abraham declares his faith in God, *"God will provide Himself a lamb."* Some versions change that around and read, "God *himself* will provide a lamb," which is also true and beautiful. But, think about this verse in relation to our need of a savior. Abraham said, "God will provide Himself," and He did. At exactly the right time in history, God sent His son, Jesus—the Lamb of God who takes away the sin of the world. John 1:29 NLT.

Dear one, our greatest need in life is to be restored to God.

We can't fix that problem with a fig leaf or an animal skin, a foreman or a set of blueprints. Our best efforts are in vain. He is Holy and our sin prevents us from restoring or initiating relationship with Him. We need help. We need a Savior. Our best efforts always fall short because—all have sinned and fall short of the glory of God. Romans 3:23 KJV.

So He stepped in. God provided "Himself", through His Incarnation in Jesus Christ, to repair the breach that sin had caused.

> For the wages of sin is death; but the gift of God is eternal life through Jesus Christ our Lord. Romans 6:23 KJV

Through Christ the Father provided Himself as the sacrificial Lamb, and now we are saved from the consequences of sin and restored to relationship with God through the Messiah, Jesus Christ.

Nor is there salvation in any other, for there is no other name under heaven given among men by which we must be saved.

Acts 4:12 KJV.

Genesis is the book of beginnings; the beginning of the world, the beginning of mankind and the beginning of selfish choices that revealed our greatest need—one only God could meet. And, He did, through the Lord and Savior, Jesus Christ, the One we all need.

--- *The Book Of* ---

EXODUS

God sees,
hears and
knows

Then the Lord said,

I have surely seen the affliction of my people... and have heard their cry... I know their sufferings, and I am come down to deliver them... Exodus 3:7-8 KJV

In Genesis, we read the story of Abraham's family including his descendants, Isaac, Isaac's twin son's, Jacob and Esau, and Jacob's twelve sons who would become the twelve tribes of Israel. Toward the end of the Genesis, we read the story of Joseph, one of Jacob's sons, who had been wronged by his brothers and wound up in Egypt where God blessed him. Joseph became one of Pharaoh's trusted leaders, and, ultimately, literally saved his father's entire family during a famine as all of Israel moved to Egypt where they worked, farmed and established lives for themselves. Life was pretty good for Israel for many years.

The book of Exodus begins when, long after Joseph died, and a series of leaders rotated through the top spot in Egypt, a Pharaoh arose who didn't remember Joseph. This man was threatened by the size and strength of Israel so he sought to make life as tough on them as possible. Ultimately, he tried to control their population growth by killing all newborn baby boys.

The people of Israel cried out to God in their affliction, and God knew it was time for their deliverance. He enacted a plan by saving a little boy who had been born to a very clever mother. The boy was spared and even raised in Pharaoh's household with his own mother as his nursemaid! The boy's name was Moses.

Moses became like a son to Pharaoh until God, from a burning bush, recruited Moses. God delivered Israel from the affliction of Egypt through the process of Moses convincing Pharaoh to let the people of God go their way. It wasn't easy. Israel was a solid workforce, and Pharaoh was reluctant. So God sent a series of ten plagues to soften Pharaoh's heart, which culminated with the final plague, the death of the first born of each home in Egypt. Since Israel was in Egypt then they would experience the terror of the plague as well, but God instituted a plan whereby they would be safe, literally 'passed over' by the angel of death as it moved through the country.

Passover

God gave specific instructions to Israel for the night the angel of death would pass over the land. What God instituted became known as "The Passover" and included every family eating dinner a certain way and wiping the blood of a lamb on the doorposts of their home so the angel of death would pass over that house. In the end, the children of Israel were spared what the people of Egypt woke up to the next morning, the death of the firstborn in every home. With this tragic turn, Pharaoh not only allowed, but, demanded, that Moses take the people and leave - and they did. Immediately.

The Passover, still celebrated today, is a symbol of the Messiah, Jesus Christ, God's Passover Lamb, protecting His people who are under the blood of the sacrificial Lamb.

Having been covered by the blood of the lamb, the children of Israel leave town but are subsequently chased by Pharaoh, who once again hardened his heart. With their backs against the Red Sea, God sealed their freedom and Pharaoh's fate by opening a pathway across the sea on dry land. When Pharaoh tried to follow the same path, God released the waters, causing Pharaoh and his army to perish in the waves.

Israel's crossing of the Red Sea is a symbol of New Testament baptism. The Apostle Paul writes:

I don't want you to forget, dear brothers and sisters, about our ancestors in the wilderness long ago. All of them were guided by a cloud that moved ahead of them, and all of them walked through the sea on dry ground. In the cloud and in the sea, all of them were baptized as followers of Moses. 1 Corinthians 10:1-2 NLT

Baptism is how God effects our deliverance from sin and entry into His eternal kingdom.

Beginning in Exodus chapter twenty, God calls Moses to meet Him on Mt. Sinai where He dictates His Law, starting with the Ten Commandments. God makes clear through the Law that He did not set the people free from Egypt to run amok and do their own thing. They were free from slavery and bondage, but it was a freedom with boundaries, primarily, freedom under God's rule.

They were delivered from bondage to boundaries.

Unchecked freedom is never handled well by humans so God outlined a kind of framework for life in His Kingdom. And, when Jesus, God Incarnate, came to earth, He didn't abolish the Old Covenant law. In fact, Jesus said:

Think not that I am come to destroy the law, or the prophets: I am not come to destroy, but to fulfil. Matthew 5:17 KJV

The Apostle Paul sheds more light on Christ and the Law when he says:

Let me put it another way. The law was our guardian until Christ came; it protected us until we could be made right with God through faith. And now that the way of faith has come, we no longer need the law as our guardian. For you are all children of God through faith in Christ Jesus. And all who have been united with

Christ in baptism have put on Christ, like putting on new clothes. There is no longer Jew or Gentile, slave or free, male and female. For you are all one in Christ Jesus. And now that you belong to Christ, you are the true children of Abraham. You are his heirs, and God's promise to Abraham belongs to you. Galatians 3:24-29 NLT

God also gave Moses instructions for how His presence would be manifest among them during the wilderness journey. He provided plans for a structure, a kind of tent, called a tabernacle, that would be shuttled from place to place. When the Tabernacle was assembled, God's presence would descend in the form of a cloud assuring the people that He was in their midst. And, when it was time for them to pack up and travel, the cloud would lift. Then, at night, a flame of fire would lead them.

In like manner, in the New Testament, after Jesus' victorious resurrection and ascension back to heaven, the Holy Spirit came to be with, and in, each believer, a seal and sign of the presence of God in our lives. As with the Tabernacle, it's not so much about a specific location, but He goes with us, and we go with Him, following the leading and the will of our heavenly King like a "cloud by day and a fire by night."

Dear one, God sees you, He hears you, and He knows your deepest needs. Call out for deliverance today, He is mighty to save.

--- *the* Book *of* ---

LEVITICUS

how to
be
holy

And the Lord spoke...

to Moses, saying, 'Speak to all the congregation of the people of Israel and say to them, You shall be holy, for I the Lord your God am holy.' Leviticus 19:1-2 NKJV

Leviticus provides details for how the worship of God should be conducted among the children of Israel, and it is very specific. Detailed in the same way NASA might detail a mission to Mars, with the torque of every bolt and exacting measurements and equations of each system. A spacecraft has to be perfect, or it won't make it home. Leviticus suggests the same thing about approaching God; it has to be perfect, and Leviticus is God's guidebook or blueprint for doing it right.

In fact, when Jesus Christ, the Son of God, came to earth, centuries later, He echoed the same sentiment: 'You, therefore, must be perfect, as your heavenly Father is perfect.' Matthew 5:48 ESV

Reading Leviticus, you may be absolutely overwhelmed with minute details. Everything has to be precise. Exact. And, of course, this is how the worship of God should be if you think about it, because He is God, after all.

As David sang in his "Song of Deliverance":

God's way is perfect. All the Lord's promises prove true. He is a shield for all who look to him for protection. 2 Samuel 22:31 NLT

God's way is perfect, He is perfect. But for us, perfection is out of reach. We tend to get in our own way. You may surmise while reading Leviticus that God must be in heaven with some kind of scorecard and a red pen, just waiting for people to mess up so He has a reason to flunk them, like that teacher most of us had in school, who could always find something we could have done better.

But, God isn't sitting on a cloud keeping score. This is where the Pharisees in the New Testament missed the mark completely, by trying to follow each directive of the Law in the most minute detail while missing the entire point, which is He is holy and He wants us to be like Him.

He is holy and He wants us to be like Him.

God's plan for the children of Israel to worship Him rightly was possible only through the system He devised and provided to Moses. It involved three things: Priests, Offerings, and Obedience.

Priests

The priests were individuals set apart to God, who conducted the sacrifices, offerings and rituals on behalf of the nation and were led by the High Priest, who represented the people before God. Only the High Priest was allowed in the holy places of the Tabernacle, and then only under specific terms. In the New Covenant, Jesus is our Great High Priest, who was tempted in every way we are, yet remained without sin, and by His sacrificial death, burial and resurrection, became the one mediator between man and God, fulfilling the role of the Levitical High Priest.

> Seeing then that we have a great High Priest who has passed through the heavens, Jesus the Son of God, let us hold fast our confession. For we do not have a High Priest who cannot sympathize with our weaknesses, but was in all points tempted as we are, yet without sin. Let us therefore come boldly to the throne of grace, that we may obtain mercy and find grace to help in time of need. Hebrews 4:14-16 NKJV

Offerings

Five different offerings to God are outlined at the beginning of Leviticus as a sort of gift of worship God would receive and, in return, extend the grace and mercy needed to cover the sins of those bringing the gift.

In the New Testament, John the Baptist rightly identified Jesus as -

The Lamb of God who takes away the sins of the world!

John: 1:29 NKJV

Jesus gave Himself as the once-for-all sacrifice, fulfilling the temporary nature of the Levitical offerings with His own blood, as Peter wrote:

But with the precious blood of Christ, as of a lamb without blemish and without spot. 1 Peter 1:19 KJV

Now we bring our gift of worship to God by faith, through the finished work of Jesus Christ, the Lamb of God.

Obedience

The Law and Commandments were directives, not suggestions, and the only way the priests could truly represent the people, and God could govern as Lord and King, were through the obedience of the nation, corporately and individually. Obedience was the key. It still is. It is no different in the new covenant where we come to Jesus by faith, and receive by grace, His gift of salvation and forgiveness for our sins. Then, flowing from our love for God, we seek to live, not in strict obedience to the Law of Moses, but in simple obedience to His Word. Jesus said:

If you love me, keep my commandments. John 14:15 NKJV

We don't obey His commands because obedience is an end in itself. We obey out of love because we want to be like Him. Jesus was the supreme example of Holiness, and His life is what God meant when He told the children of Israel:

You shall be holy, for I, the Lord your God am Holy.

Leviticus 19:2 NKJV

Dear one, when you read Leviticus, realize that God's desire for you is to be holy, which is to be like Jesus, and for your life to exhibit holiness, that comes from purity of mind and motive, selfless giving, heartfelt adoration and love for God, love for all people and remorse for sin.

--- the Book of ---

NUMBERS

He remains
faithful

This is a trustworthy

saying:

If we die with him, we will also live with him.

If we endure hardship, we will reign with him.

If we deny him, he will deny us.

If we are unfaithful, he remains faithful,

for he cannot deny who he is. 2 Timothy 2:11-13 NLT.

The book of Numbers, the fourth book of the Law, is a story about the wilderness. The wilderness is always a proving ground that separates who you think you are, from who you really are. You can't hide from yourself in the wilderness. The wilderness divides what you think from what you know, belief from unbelief. This is as true today as it was for Moses, Aaron and the people of Israel.

Israel had been miraculously delivered from bondage in Egypt when God parted the Red Sea and literally baptized them all through the water, swallowing Pharaoh in the wake, and giving God's people what they had been crying out to Him for on the other side—freedom.

But it wouldn't be a freedom of selfish anarchy. It would be freedom under the Lordship of their true King, God. And God gave them instructions for how to live and details for how to honor Him in worship. He dwelt in their midst, and they were safe, free, guided, governed and on their way to the promised land, the place of destiny and blessing.

But they never made it.

At least, the first generation didn't, because of their unbelief. The wilderness revealed their hearts. The wilderness will do that. When physical, mental and emotional pressure come from change, or people, or difficult circumstances, some will want to turn around and run back to what is known, even if it is unpleasant. They would rather return to bondage than walk forward in a difficult victory. So, they murmur, they complain, they undermine and grumble.

So God told Moses, "I will pardon them as you have requested. But as surely as I live, and as surely as the earth is filled with the Lord's glory, not one of these people will ever enter that land. They have all seen my glorious presence and the miraculous signs I performed both in Egypt and in the wilderness, but again and again, they have tested me by refusing to listen to my voice." Numbers 14:20-22 NLT.

So God reserved the Promised Land for the next generation, the youngsters whose faith was not spoiled, those who believed in the impossible, the ones who would listen to God and obey His voice, while the first generation perished in the desert.

But, God still loved them, that never changed, even in the midst of nearly universal unfaithfulness, God remained faithful.

His presence remained in the Tabernacle, and He provided for Israel daily, even in small, personal details, like their shoes never wearing out. Little glimpses of the loving provision that would remind anyone with eyes to see and ears to hear that He was with them, and He was for them.

The writer of Hebrews recounts the wilderness story of Numbers and uses it to encourage us to remain faithful to the end. He writes:

Be careful then, dear brothers and sisters. Make sure that your own hearts are not evil and unbelieving, turning you away from the living God. You must warn each other every day, while it is still "today," so that none of you will be deceived by sin and hardened against God. For if we are faithful to the end, trusting God just as firmly as when we first believed, we will share in all that belongs to Christ. Remember what it says:

Today when you hear his voice, don't harden your hearts as Israel did when they rebelled.' And who was it who rebelled against God, even though they heard his voice? Wasn't it the people Moses led out of Egypt? And who made God angry for forty years? Wasn't it the people who sinned, whose corpses lay in the wilderness? And to whom was God speaking when he took an oath that they would never enter his rest? Wasn't it the people who disobeyed him? So we see that because of their unbelief they were not able to enter his rest. Hebrews 3: 12-19 NLT.

Dear one, if you are in the wilderness right now, take heart, God is near to you. He will never leave you or forsake you. Remain faithful. If you are murmuring, complaining, even wishing you could go back to bondage, stop. Repent. Those feelings are lies. Keep your heart tender. Because up ahead is the land of promise, the place of rest. Satan wants to rob you of your destiny through unbelief. But God is faithful. Let Him take you there.

P.S. Hebrews chapter 3 and 4 provide amazing New Testament context to the book of Numbers. Try and read these two chapters before you start Numbers and immediately after you finish. You'll find how beautifully this book relates to our life in Christ.

--- *the Book of* ---

DEUTERONOMY

When the
End is the
Beginning

God is Faithful

Therefore know that the Lord your God, He is God, the faithful God who keeps covenant and mercy for a thousand generations with those who love Him and keep His commandments.

Deuteronomy 7:9 NKJV

A thousand generations is a long time. Moses is probably using an enormous number like that to signify that God's steadfast love and faithfulness to His Word goes on forever. But, think about it—if a generation is about 40 years, then 1,000 generations would be 40,000 years. If Abraham's covenant with God was about 4,000 years ago, and the new covenant of Jesus Christ about 2,000 years ago, then you can see - God's faithfulness to His Word is just getting started!

Not that you or I will be around in 36,000 years, but whatever things look like, God's faithfulness and love will be the same because He doesn't change, as Moses wrote here, "The Lord our God is God," and later in the Old Testament, "I am the Lord, I do not change ..." Malachi 3:6 NLT. Then, as it is written in the New Testament about God the Son:

Jesus Christ is the same, yesterday, today and forever.

Hebrews 13:8 NLT

It is good news that God's love and faithfulness last forever because it means that what seems like the end isn't always the end; sometimes it is just the beginning.

When Moses finished Deuteronomy and was giving his final charge to Joshua and the new leaders, he was about 120 years old. Moses' life was nearing the end—but the foundation he had established for the future of Israel was just beginning.

Here in Deuteronomy we begin to see a cyclical outline common to all of human history that God reveals in the Five Books of the Law. God's dealing with mankind tends to follow a predictable, repeating pattern. It goes kind of like this:

Genesis

We all need. Genesis shows us that one constant among people is that we all need something we cannot supply on our own, usually to be delivered from problems of our own making. It's not a bad thing if we know where to look for help. Mankind's main problem is looking for help in all the wrong places. But, God always supplies what we lack. He meets our need.

Exodus

God Sees, Hears and Knows. He knows our needs, both the smallest needs that are only important personally, and we think no one notices, and our greatest need, deliverance from bondage to sin. God is our Deliverer.

Leviticus

How to Be Holy. God sees our need, provides our deliverance, and calls us to be holy as He is Holy. And since our selfish minds could never figure out what God's holiness would look like in practice, He gives a blueprint to follow with the law and commandments, the definitive way to worship and conduct oneself, down to the very letter. But, keeping the letter of the law is difficult, or rather, impossible, and through trying in vain, we discover our weakness.

Numbers

He Remains Faithful. The law exposes our sinfulness and we realize how incapable we really are, even with the best of intentions, of keeping the law in a holy way. This leads to frustration, disobedience, unbelief and wandering around in a wilderness never meant for us. But, God does not leave, even when we deny Him, because He can't deny Himself, He is faithful.

Deuteronomy

When the End is the Beginning. The word Deuteronomy means "second law" and it is essentially the retelling of the law to the new generation of Israelites, who had grown up in the wilderness. However, instead of responding like their fathers, with fleshly overconfidence, they received the law with the understanding of their own limitations based on what they had seen their parents go through. And this was right where God wanted them—where He had wanted the nation from day one— at a place where they were truly ready for Him to lead. And grace began to flow over their lives. And the children of Israel began again. The wilderness wasn't the end of the story.

Moses passed the leadership of the people over to Joshua, whose name is the Hebrew word for Jesus.

Joshua is a type or symbol of Christ in that he leads the people, in God's strength, into their land of promise.

You can't force your way into the promised land, dear one. You won't get there until you stop trying so hard. Eventually, you realize this and surrender. But, you don't surrender to failure. You surrender to God. Then, what may have seemed like the end, turns out to be an exciting new beginning—and He will lead you in.

--- *the Book of* ---

JOSHUA

there
is
more

When Joshua...

was an old man, the Lord said to him, "You are growing old, and much land remains to be conquered."
Joshua 13:1 NLT.

The Book of Joshua is the story of the children of Israel crossing the Jordan River and entering the land of promise. Finally, after 40 years of wandering in the desert, Moses, through whom the law was given, took them as far as he could, but he could not bring them in. Joshua, who is a type of Christ, whose name means salvation, and is the Hebrew word for Jesus, would finish what Moses started.

God delivered Israel from bondage in Egypt, and that would have been enough, but He had more for them. He had a land of promise. This is the wonder of God, that He doesn't just forgive our sins and remove our guilt and shame. The free gift of salvation in Jesus Christ doesn't end with the deliverance from bondage to sin—there is an entering in to promise!

This is our boundless inheritance in Christ.

Moses leads them out (of bondage) and Joshua leads them in (to promise).

The first thing they experience on the other side of the river is the imposing fortress of Jericho, and progress stops. They can't go around it, they can't go through it, and they can't make it go away. Jericho is unconquerable with walls 100 feet high and 30 feet thick. Jericho represents the super-obstacles in our lives that halt our progress and prevent us from moving forward, roadblocks that taunt us and mock our weakness. Things like sickness, poverty, addiction, disability, or obesity - "You made it this far, but this is where you stop. You lose! I win again!" the super-obstacle mocks.

But God has other plans, plans for victory and not defeat, plans for conquest and blessing. He tore down the walls and gave them the city through completely unexpected means.

There is more to salvation than deliverance. There is the promise of wholeness, which is a definition of being saved, being made whole; body, mind, and spirit. Salvation is being restored to relationship with God, a relationship that had been forfeited to sin.

By God's grace, the super-obstacles in our lives will fall before the One who conquered sin, death and the grave and now leads His children into the promised land, and nothing can stop Him.

Here is how the Apostle Paul describes it in Romans chapter eight:

> The law of Moses was unable to save us because of the weakness of our sinful nature. So God did what the law could not do. He sent his own Son in a body like the bodies we sinners have. And in that body God declared an end to sin's control over us by giving his Son as a sacrifice for our sins. He did this so that the just requirement of the law would be fully satisfied for us, who no longer follow our sinful nature but instead follow the Spirit...

What shall we say about such wonderful things as these? If God is for us, who can ever be against us? Since he did not spare even his own Son but gave him up for us all, won't he also give us everything else? Who dares accuse us whom God has chosen for his own? No one—for God himself has given us right standing with himself. Who then will condemn us? No one—for Christ Jesus died for us and was raised to life for us, and he is sitting in the place of honor at God's right hand, pleading for us...

Can anything ever separate us from Christ's love? ... No power in the sky above or in the earth below—indeed, nothing in all creation will ever be able to separate us from the love of God that is revealed in Christ Jesus our Lord. Romans 8: 3-4, 31-34, 38a,39 NLT.

This is the power that fueled Joshua and led the children of Israel to march through the super-obstacle of Jericho and possess the land. And it doesn't stop.

But, sometimes life's circumstances can nudge us to stop, to settle or slow our forward progress. That's why we must be careful and keep listening to the Lord. Joshua accomplished more than almost anyone in history, and when he got old and tired, God spoke to him...

Now Joshua was old and advanced in years, and the LORD said to him, 'You are old and advanced in years, and there remains yet very much land to possess. Joshua 13:1 NKJV.

Well past the age of retirement, creaky knees and a sore back, Joshua was ready for a cool glass of iced tea and a chaise lounge; but God basically said, "I know you're old, but there's more to do."

So Joshua kept moving forward.

It's the same for us, dear one. There is always more, not in the sense of physical movement or accumulation of things, but in learning to love, denying our self, building character, mining wisdom and being conformed into the image of Christ, growing more intimate with God day by day, and ultimately, as the Apostle Peter wrote, becoming partakers of the divine nature.

> **By which have been given to us exceedingly great and precious promises, that through these you may be partakers of the divine nature, having escaped the corruption that is in the world through lust. 2 Peter 1:4 NKJV.**

God longs to draw each of us deeper into the land of promise, deeper into relationship with Him. Have you reached the end? Are you there yet? No. Should you stop? No. There remains much to conquer.

--- *the* B o o k *of* ---

JUDGES

He

never

left

Then the children

of Israel did evil in the sight of the Lord, and served the Baals; and they forsook the Lord God of their fathers, who had brought them out of the land of Egypt; and they followed other gods from among the gods of the people who were all around them, and they bowed down to them; and they provoked the Lord to anger. They forsook the Lord and served Baal and the Ashtoreths. Judges 2:11-13 NKJV

Joshua led Israel into the Promised Land, and they quickly established themselves, moving through the region, conquering city after city. Joshua was aged, probably in his eighties, when they started the quest. He led the people into the land, ultimately dividing the territories between the twelve families (Jacob/Israel's sons, the twelve tribes of Israel), until he died at the age of 110. (Judges 2:8).

Unfortunately, after Joshua and his generation died, the next generation failed to maintain the allegiance to God in obedience to the law. In fact, the prophet Samuel, the probable author of Judges, writes that they forgot the Lord and all He had done for Israel.

After that generation died, another generation grew up who did not acknowledge the Lord or remember the mighty things he had done for Israel.

Judges 2:10 NLT

And, sadly, because the children of Israel had forgotten God, the theme of Judges, a book that spans 300 years of history, is a repeating cycle of Israel's disobedience, defeat, discipline and deliverance.

The era of the Judges were like smaller, local versions of the bondage in Egypt played out again and again.

Israel would reject God and be routed by some invading force that would make life miserable for them. Eventually, they cried out to God from oppression, and God would send a judge, Gideon or Samson or a number of others through the years, to deliver them. They would be set free and give Him thanks. Then, before you know it, they disobeyed again, forsook Him again, and God allowed them to reap the consequences of their sin. He delivered them into the enemies' hand until they could take no more and cried out to Him, and He sent a deliverer. The cycle continued, like a dog chasing its tail.

How quickly we forget what God has done. God can do a great miracle of deliverance in our life, save us from injury or provide miraculously and we will be literally aglow with His praise. But, then a little trouble comes, a late notice, a diagnosis, a layoff, and our arms drop, and our shoulders slump, and we lower our face and say "Woe is me." And pretty soon we're bowing down to another idol, putting our hope in something or someone other than God. And we walk away, trying to fix things in our own strength, only to make it worse.

Eventually we reach the end of ourselves and cry out to Him, and guess what? We find Him waiting for us. We find He was right here all along. He never left. He is ever near, ever patient, mighty to save.

Why do we have such short memories when it comes to what God has done? Hasn't He proven Himself faithful?

Has He not embraced us with love like no other? Didn't He pull us out of a pit of our own making and set our feet on a solid rock? Yes! Yes! Yes!

We must cultivate remembrance, review His blessing, recount with our children and grandchildren His goodness and the great things He has done - so we won't forget, and so they won't forget! When the pressure is on they can turn to Him and cry out knowing He will be there for them, as He was for their parents and grandparents.

For the children of Israel, their excuse comes in the last verse of Judges. Samuel inadvertently waits till the very end and reveals the core issue:

> **In those days there was no king in Israel; everyone did what was right in his own eyes. Judges 21:25 NKJV.**

They had a King, God. Israel was a Theocracy. Only they did not honor God as King, and they disregarded the laws and safeguards He had put in place for the nation. But without acknowledging an objective standard, a moral code of right and wrong that is universally adhered to, people resort to looking out for themselves, living world views of their own making based on convenience, selfishness and power. Selfish, sinful people tend to walk away from God, instead of toward Him, so they avoid His loving standard.

Our country is a mess, not because the wrong side of the aisle is in power, but because we have forgotten God. Politics can't fix that.

Dear one, the only cure for having left God is repentance, both individually and corporately, changing our direction, crying out to Him for deliverance, and you know what we would find? He is there, He never left, He never will. He is God; He is love; He is mighty to save. Put your hope in Him and Him alone.

--- *the Book of* ---

RUTH

my Redeemer lives

In historical context,

the story of Ruth takes place concurrently with the last few chapters of Judges, which were some of the darkest days in the history of Israel. People had forgotten God and were just doing what was right in their own eyes. And, what is right in most people's eyes is self-preservation at any cost, which equaled a sad and selfish period of rebellion against God.

Against the backdrop of darkness, this little story of hope is taking place in the small town of Bethlehem among the people of Judah and the family of Elimelech.

Ruth is a parenthesis of light in an otherwise dark chapter of history.

As the story goes, Elimelech takes his wife, Naomi, and two sons to Moab during a time of famine, leaving the safety of his people and village, which was unadvised. However, in those days everyone, including Elimelech, was just doing what they thought was right for themselves. While in Moab, the two boys married Moabite women, also something the people of Israel were not supposed to do.

Elimelech soon died, and a few years later, the two sons also died leaving their mother, Naomi alone in a foreign country with her two daughters in law, Orpah and Ruth, both Moabites. Orpah returned to her people, but Ruth decided to stay with Naomi and committed herself to her mother in law for life. Her beautiful vow of allegiance to her mother-in-law is written in the first chapter where Ruth said:

> Entreat me not to leave you, Or to turn back from following after you; For wherever you go, I will go; And wherever you lodge, I will lodge; Your people shall be my people, And your God, my God.

Where you die, I will die, And there will I be buried. The Lord do so to me, and more also, If anything but death parts you and me." Ruth 1:16-17 NKJV

So Naomi and Ruth returned to Israel, the elder, Naomi, having lost her husband and sons while away. She told the people of Bethlehem, **"I went away full, but the Lord has brought me home empty." Ruth 1:21 NLT.** What a solemn homecoming she must have had.

Since Elimelech had died, his inheritance could be passed to the nearest relative if any met the qualifications of redemption, which, in addition to property, included marrying Ruth, whose husband had died before having children and extending the family name. Elimelech's closest relative was unable to fulfill the requirements, so the opportunity fell to another relative of Elimelech, Boaz.

Boaz didn't have to redeem them; he chose to redeem them. He didn't need the land, but he loved Ruth, having found her to be kind and virtuous. So Boaz set about to do anything he could to secure the redemption of Elimelech's house that he might marry Ruth.

The ancient custom of the kinsman redeemer is revisited in Revelation chapter five, where we see a scroll in the right hand of God which seemingly contains the mysteries of God's judgment and salvation. It is sealed with seven seals, and no one in heaven or earth is found who is worthy to open the scroll. There is no apparent kinsman who meets the requirements.

Then Jesus appears in the scene as the Lamb of God and receives the scroll, the audience around the throne then bows down, rejoicing, singing a new song:

You are worthy to take the scroll, And to open its seals; For You were slain, And have redeemed us to God by Your blood out of every tribe and tongue and people and nation... Revelation 5:9 NKJV

The first book of Samuel falls, historically, toward the end of Judges. Samuel himself was probably born while Samson was Judge of Israel. It was a transitional period in Israel's history as the time of the Judges ending after a span of around 300 years, and the people of Israel finally getting the king they had been asking for.

God appointed Samuel as prophet, judge and priest. He was born in answer to his mother's prayers and dedicated to God before his conception.

> So Samuel grew, and the Lord was with him and let none of his words fall to the ground. And all Israel from Dan to Beersheba knew that Samuel had been established as a prophet of the Lord.
>
> 1 Samuel 3:19-20 NKJV

Of how many people could it be said: "(he) let none of God's words fall to the ground?" Precious few, I imagine. Samuel valued the word of God and was careful with what God said.

In addition to Samuel, the other main character in 1 Samuel is Saul, the first king of Israel. Samuel gave the people a message from God, warning them it was a mistake to desire a king, but they wouldn't listen.

> Nevertheless the people refused to obey the voice of Samuel; and they said, "No, but we will have a king over us, that we also may be like all the nations, and that our king may judge us and go out before us and fight our battles."
>
> 1 Samuel 8:19-20 NKJV

In other words, we want someone to follow. Everyone can't be the leader, so we want one to be king over us. The problem was that they already had a leader and king, God Almighty, Who had delivered them out of captivity, led them through the wilderness and always responded to their cries even through seasons of disobedience—but that wasn't enough.

Following God is hard, blaming God is impossible.

And that is sometimes what we do. We want to follow someone to relieve our own personal responsibility. If we just do what the King says, then mistakes are his fault, not ours. If it wasn't for God's unfailing love, the ensuing time of Kings would have completely derailed Israel, because while there were some very good kings; there were also some very bad ones.

Wanting someone to follow and, ultimately, someone to blame, is a challenge in the Christian life as well. When we enter into God's kingdom through faith in the sufficiency of Christ to forgive our guilt and the penalty for our sin, we enter into a new kingdom where Christ is King. We return, in a sense, to live under the rulership of someone we cannot see. He has given us His infallible Word and promised to dwell within us by His Spirit, Who guides, comforts, teaches and intercedes for us. But, that doesn't make the Christian walk easy.

The Word challenges us continually to deny ourselves and be better than we are by making choices that honor God, serving, loving, resisting powerful urges to conform, judge, slack off. Jesus said:

> **Because narrow is the gate and difficult is the way which leads to life, and there are few who find it. Matthew 7:14 NKJV**

Take a look at the fragmented church today. You can probably find one or a dozen that routinely justify behavior that is biblically wrong, conforming instead to a broken and blinded culture of selfishness. And, their leaders seem to justify it all and twist scripture to make it say what they want. Some of this lazy theology would make it a lot easier to be a Christian because there is really no distinction between them and the world at large. Let's make it a casual, social, gospel. Ah, easy. And if it's wrong, oh well, I'm just a follower, it's leaderships fault, I'm just following their lead.

But that kind of easy abdication of responsibility doesn't work in actual practice, because Christianity is personal. Your relationship with God is first personal, then communal. You are accountable for both what you know, what you do, and what He has said in His Word. If you hear a leader explaining away a passage of scripture to mean the opposite of what it obviously says, it's on you whether you sit still for it or not.

Instead of looking to a king, like Saul, someone to blame for our mistakes and relieve our personal responsibility to change and be change agents in our culture, let us desire, instead, to be like Samuel, to be someone of whom it could be said, he "let none of [God's] words fall to the ground."

2 SAMUEL & 1 CHRONICLES

remember who you are

Now these are...

the last words of David.

Thus says David the son of Jesse; Thus says the man raised up on high, The anointed of the God of Jacob, And the sweet psalmist of Israel. 2 Samuel 23:1

The books of 2 Samuel and 1 Chronicles cover the life of King David. Samuel wrote 2 Samuel just after the events he describes transpired. Ezra likely authored 1 Chronicles many years later, expanding on stories from the books of Samuel and Kings. Both books, though, follow the life of King David, one of the greatest leaders in history and one called **"a man after God's own heart."** (Acts 13:22)

David had a simple and yet profound trust and love for God which revealed itself in his life in courage and fearlessness. Whether facing the giant, Goliath, or the entire Philistine army, he always moved in the confidence of God. David knew who he was. In fact, his last words, transcribed in 2 Samuel 23, begin with him revealing his heart, calling himself *"the man God raised up, or exalted; the anointed of God, the sweet psalmist of Israel."* This is who he was.

For the most part, his life is a reflection of who he was at his core, but there were times he forgot Who had called and enabled him to lead. He forgot the core reality of who God had raised him up to be. David gave in to the lusts of the flesh and the power that his calling had granted him. One such time is recorded in chapter eleven where it says:

It happened in the spring of the year, at the time when kings go out to battle, that David sent Joab and his servants with him, and all Israel; and they destroyed the people of Ammon and besieged Rabbah. But David remained at Jerusalem. 2 Samuel 11:1 NKJV

David was king and as Samuel records it here, this was a time kings took their place in the field and led their armies, as David himself had always done. But this time he stayed behind; the text doesn't say why. But while he was at home in Jerusalem, and not where he should have been, he found himself on his roof where he saw a young woman bathing. David inquired about her, sent for her and committed adultery with her—because she was married to a man in David's own military service. The young woman conceived leading David to arrange for her husband to be placed on the front lines, effectively sending him to his death. Lust, adultery, murder. Why?

David forgot who he was. Vocationally he was king. As such he had a job to do. He was called to shepherd Israel, and, this time of year, that meant lead the troops. But even deeper than his calling was his core. He was a man of faith and depth, the sweet psalmist, raised up and anointed of God.

Forgetting who you are will lead to distraction, sin, and consequences.

I often tell my children and my grandchildren before they compete, go to school or venture out with friends, "Remember who you are." In the immediate context, I am telling them that whatever they encounter to remember that we are part of each other, my blood flows through their veins, they represent our family, our integrity, our honor. And, personally, I am telling them to remember they are Christian, they are not their own, they have been bought with the precious blood of Jesus Christ and are ambassadors for Christ—they represent their Lord.

Everything we do or say will be a reflection of our calling and our core. Satan would like to distract you with the lusts of the flesh and trip you, get you to be something that you are not. Don't fall for it.

Like David, you are someone's son:

He was the son of Jesse. Jesse's blood coursed through David's veins, and David represented his father and his family. My dad wasn't perfect, but I honor him and the name he gave me. My children don't have a perfect father, but their lives reflect a better me.

Some people don't know their earthly father, some have nothing but bad experiences with their parents, but we all can do this; we can thank God for life and the opportunity to know a Heavenly Father Who will be to us everything our biological father's or mother's could not be.

Like David, you have been "raised up" by God:

> If then you were raised with Christ, seek those things which are above, where Christ is, sitting at the right hand of God. Set your mind on things above, not on things on the earth.
> Colossians 3:1-2 NKJV

Like David, you have been "anointed" by God:

> But the anointing which you have received from Him abides in you… 1 John 2:27. This is the seal of the Holy Spirit.

Like David, you are a "sweet psalmist" of God:

Now, not all of us sing or write poetry, but all of us communicate somehow, usually by conversation, and that conversation should reflect the beauty, goodness and love of God.

This is who you are, loved one, if you are a Christian. This is your core. Remember who you are.

--- *the* B o o k *of* ---

1 KINGS &
2 CHRONICLES

the

opposite of

love

1 and 2 Kings,

and 2 Chronicles cover the same period of history, with 1 Kings reflected in the first part of 2 Chronicles and 2 Kings in the second half.

1 Kings details the life of Solomon, David's son, who inherited the throne from his father and became the envy of the entire world, amassing wealth untold and governing with unsurpassed wisdom and knowledge. The second half of the book describes the division of the kingdom which had been united for over seventy years under David and Solomon.

Solomon was a great king and accomplished the building of the temple that his father had dreamed about as well as achieving a level of peace in the country that was uncommon in those days. Solomon also carved out time to author several books including much of the Proverbs, Song of Solomon and Ecclesiastes. But with all his wisdom and achievement, he retained a blindspot in his life that would ultimately spell his undoing. We get a glimpse of it in chapter three.

> **Solomon made an alliance with Pharaoh, the king of Egypt, and married one of his daughters. He brought her to live in the City of David until he could finish building his palace and the Temple of the Lord and the wall around the city. 1 Kings 3:1 NLT**

As wonderful and grand as the temple was when completed, it is interesting to note that prior to that Solomon focused almost twice as long on building his own palace. 1 Kings 6:38 and 7:1 record that he spent thirteen years on his palace and seven years on the temple. Does that seem a little out of balance?

Solomon loved the Lord his God, but He also loved himself to an unhealthy extent, even when what he wanted went against God's word.

> Now King Solomon loved many foreign women…The Lord had clearly instructed the people of Israel, "You must not marry them, because they will turn your hearts to their gods." Yet Solomon insisted on loving them anyway. He had 700 wives of royal birth and 300 concubines. And in fact, they did turn his heart away from the Lord. 1 Kings 11:1-3 NLT

To say Solomon pampered himself with whatever he wanted would be an understatement. As you read through 1 Kings, you see an accumulation of riches that defies understanding.

Self-love is a deceptive thing.

Much of modern theology promotes a Solomon-esque type of self-love. One of loving yourself, pampering yourself, satisfying your every desire and comfort. But this type of love isn't biblical. The kind of self "love" the Bible talks about is taking care of basic needs and not abusing ourselves. When our body is hungry, we eat. Thirsty, we drink. Cold, seek shelter. This is in keeping with Jesus' mandate to love our neighbor as ourselves; when we see one hungry or thirsty or hurting, we are called to minister to those needs, as we would for ourselves. That's love.

But like Solomon, we don't stop with basic care, we lavish upon ourselves. If I need shoes and find a style I like I buy a pair in every color. If I am hungry I eat, but not just to satisfy the hunger, I gorge myself with giant, unhealthy portions. Why? Because I want to. This focus on self is the core of so many of our problems and is really the opposite of love.

You might assume that the opposite of love is hate, but it isn't. The opposite of love is self-love.

Because real love is outward focused; we love God, we love people, we love our children. Love is recognizing that others possess intrinsic, God-ordained value as people, while self-love isn't concerned about others at all. In self-love we are concerned only with ourselves and our well being—maybe the well being of our family, but even then only to the extent of how their behavior might affect us. It's not myopic, it's "me-opic".

The sin of Solomon was predicted to be the chief characteristic of people in the last days. Paul wrote:

> … in the last days there will be very difficult times. For people will love only themselves and their money. They will be boastful and proud, scoffing at God, disobedient to their parents, and ungrateful. They will consider nothing sacred. 2 Timothy 3:1-2 NLT

We are living in a time of rampant, unhealthy, unchristian, self-love that has many good and well-meaning people in its evil grip. It is not love, rather, it is the opposite of love.

Dear one, don't aspire to be like Solomon in areas of wealth or power. They were his undoing and in the end, he realized it was all vanity. Instead:

> Do nothing out of selfish ambition or vain conceit. Rather, in humility value others above yourselves. Philippians 2:3 NIV

--- *the* B o o k *of* ---

2 KINGS &
2 CHRONICLES

the passionate

commitment

of the Lord

For a remnant

of my people will spread out from Jerusalem, a group of survivors from Mount Zion. The passionate commitment of the Lord of Heaven's Armies will make this happen!

2 Kings 19:31 NLT

The only way the scarlet thread of redemption could have survived the period of the Kings of Israel and Judah was the passionate commitment of the Lord. His love is so great and His commitment so strong that even in judgment, He always reserves a remnant of those who will not turn their hearts from Him no matter the cost. These people are God's light in the darkness, reminding the world that no matter how bad it gets, how bad the leadership is, how severe the famine, drought, economic crash, persecution or any apparent evil that would say otherwise—God is still on the Throne, and He is still in charge.

Oh, the books that could be written about the kings! In fact, they have been! Thirty or more prophets held forth God's truth during the time of the Kings. Many of these wrote the 2nd half of the Old Testament! The major and minor prophetic books were penned in and about the very days chronicled here in Kings, mostly 2 Kings.

The wickedness during this period of history was so bad that the Lord said:

I will wipe away the people of Jerusalem as one wipes a dish and turns it upside down. 2 Kings 21:13 NLT

How about that description of judgment?

Of all the kings of Israel and Judah that reigned after Solomon, only two are called good, King Hezekiah and his great-grandson, King Josiah. So bad was the apostasy of Israel that, in reading the books of the law, Josiah discovered the celebration of the Passover. It was totally off his radar. The most important event in Israel's history had been slowly taken for granted, then lost completely. Josiah restored the Passover celebration and everything else he could, but this is the extent to which things had fallen. Then, as soon as Josiah was gone, the people lapsed again, with leaders that disregarded the Lord, and the path of their fathers, and did whatever they pleased. Very sad.

The northern kingdom of Israel was eventually plummeted by the Assyrians who led them away captive, effectively erasing the ten tribes. Later, having learned nothing from these events, Judah, the southern kingdom, was destroyed by the Babylonians, who conquered them and took them into captivity. And, just like that, it was gone. The great dream that was Canaan's land, the land promised to Abraham and his descendants, the place Moses dreamed about and Joshua conquered, lost because of sin, unbelief and disobedience.

We wonder sometimes about the evil of the world in which we are living and how long the Lord might tarry before wiping our dish so to speak. We've read the end of the book. We know that Jesus came first as a baby born in a manger, and He said he would come again, this time as a king with a sword. People cannot continue sinking deeper and deeper into debauchery and evil without consequences. One day, we don't know when, the trumpet will sound, and Christ will come to judge the living and the dead.

The amazing thing we can learn from 2 Kings, though, in addition to judgment, is how loving and personal God is. We learn that He doesn't let people go easily, He loves each person so much that He will go to any length to save those who will turn to Him. Thirty prophets were sent to shine truth in the darkness. Some people received their word. Josiah was only eight years old when he became King of Judah, yet because of his heart for God, he was able to lead the nation back to God. Hezekiah, Josiah, Elisha and more were lights for God in a dark world!

Think of the grand scale of the evil going on in 2 Kings and realize the size of the task a prophet like Elisha was given—that of warning the nation of sin and calling them to repentance. It was a message for kings and leaders. Yet, while Elisha's calling had national implications, his main calling was to serve people, which reflects the heart of God. Once a simple woman came to Elisha who didn't have the money to pay her bills. He ministered to her, and God gave her a miracle of supply. Another time, a little boy experienced some sort of aneurysm or something and died. Elisha was far away; but when the boy's mother came to the prophet, he set aside what he was doing and went to their home. Miraculously, the boy was brought back to life.

This is the passionate commitment of the Lord. This is the God we serve. He always has a remnant of people through whom His light still shines. Beacons of love and peace who will not bow. As the prophet explained to King Asa,

> **For the eyes of the Lord run to and fro throughout the whole earth looking to show himself strong on behalf of those whose heart is perfect toward Him. 2 Chronicles 16:9 KJV**

He will show Himself strong on your behalf, dear one. Keep your heart true, keep your faith simple and pure in Jesus. No matter how bad the world gets and how much tragedy warrants His full attention, He will always be mindful of you and be there for you. His passionate commitment to you will make it happen!

--- *the* Book *of* ---

EZRA

a brief

moment of

grace

But now we

have been given a brief moment of grace, for the Lord our God has allowed a few of us to survive as a remnant.

Ezra 9:8 NLT

Ezra the priest served among the exiles to Babylon and is a giant of the faith, one of the true heroes of the Old Testament. Not only did he write most of 1 & 2 Chronicles, but also the books of Ezra, Nehemiah and probably the great Psalm 119. He was a historian and a theologian before there were such terms and eventually would lead the group of 120 that would gather the canon of the Old Testament: this is the brother whom the Lord used to help assemble the Old Testament!

Ezra served at a time when so many of the prophecies of Isaiah, Jeremiah, Ezekiel and others were coming to pass—things spoken decades and centuries before were happening all around him. Knowing Israel's history and the Books of the Law as he did, seeing the current events and the fulfillment of prophecy made Him love and trust the Lord even more.

God speaks of things that are not yet as if they are, and then they happen in the most intricate detail. Ezra doesn't just believe the promises of God, he is living in them!

Your eternal word, O Lord, stands firm in heaven. Your faithfulness extends to every generation, as enduring as the earth you created.

Psalm 119: 89-90 NLT

This is the confidence Ezra had in the Lord, and this is how he conducted his life. So when he was chosen to lead a group of exiles back to Jerusalem it says:

…the gracious hand of his God was on him… he had determined

to study and obey the law of the Lord and to teach those laws and regulations to the people of Israel. Ezra 7:9-10 NLT

What he found upon his arrival was a people who had conformed to the world around them. They hadn't repented and honored the Lord for opening the door for their return. They had learned nothing in defeat and exile. Ezra's heart was broken. He fell before the Lord and prayed:

O my God, I am utterly ashamed; I blush to lift up my face to you. For our sins are piled higher than our heads, and our guilt has reached to the heavens. From the days of our ancestors until now, we have been steeped in sin. That is why we and our kings and our priests have been at the mercy of the pagan kings of the land. We have been killed, captured, robbed, and disgraced, just as we are today. But now we have been given a brief moment of grace, for the Lord our God has allowed a few of us to survive as a remnant. Ezra 9:6-8 NLT

Dear one, like Ezra and the children of Israel, we have been given a "brief moment of grace," a moment to consider the times we have been blessed to live within, to consider how God's hand has brought us here, to consider with humility His offer of adoption as sons and daughters and the inheritance He is giving us in Christ Jesus. Will we honor Him as Lord and King? Or will we compromise with the world around us?

You don't have to wonder if God keeps His promises, you know—Jesus is His promise, kept! He is God's answer. Like Ezra, just look around. His handiwork is everywhere. His grace is all around you, behind you and before you—you're living in it. Our Promised Land isn't a geographical location, it's a person, God the Son, Jesus Christ. He is our Rock, our Fortress, our Dwelling Place and our God.

--- *the* B o o k *of* ---

NEHEMIAH

With God's help

So on October 2

the wall was finished—just fifty-two days after we had begun. When our enemies and the surrounding nations heard about it, they were frightened and humiliated. They realized this work had been done with the help of our God. Nehemiah 6:15-16 NLT

Nehemiah is the story of the rebuilding of the wall around Jerusalem that had been wrecked during the Babylonian siege. The temple had been rebuilt but the city was still exposed. Most people agreed it should be repaired but couldn't agree on anything else; they couldn't organize themselves, couldn't control the naysayers, just couldn't accomplish anything.

Word of the problems they were having made their way back to Nehemiah, also an exile from Judah, who had been elevated to special assistant to the King of Persia and now lived in the capital city. Nehemiah was an especially gifted man. He was the perfect combination of someone with a heart for God, a humble man who prayed and trusted God, and, a world-class leader, skilled in management, conflict resolution, organization, and project development.

Hearing about the situation in Jerusalem broke his heart. Leaders are often real type-a drivers who seem to operate without emotion, just doing what needs to be done for the sake of the project. Nehemiah was on a different level. He had a heart, first for God and then for God's people. Like Ezra, Nehemiah was uniquely equipped to serve during this historic, prophecy-fulfilling time in Israel's history.

Books have been written on Nehemiah's leadership style and organization, and many of today's successful leaders would have cited Nehemiah as an inspiration and key to their own success. If you have been in church for any length of time, you have probably listened to teaching on Nehemiah from pastors who sought to rally the congregation toward a common purpose, just as Nehemiah rallied the people of Jerusalem to build the wall.

Personally, I can relate more with Ezra than Nehemiah. Nehemiah had a skill set I've longed for but that eludes me. Ezra was a priest and a scribe. He was the perfect person to cover Nehemiah spiritually, to pray for him. That's more my role. I'll get out there with a hammer and trowel and pitch in as best I can, but the project overwhelms me.

Nehemiah could figure out how to use the hammer well enough to train people like me and then move on to the grand scheme. Nehemiah reminds me of my oldest daughter. She has the same humble spirit and the same God-given knack for putting things in order. Wherever she has worked, she almost instantly observes areas of inefficiency or great potential, but not only does she see them, she figures out how to fix them and make the system work better, more efficiently, more profitably. It's uncanny. It's a gift. It's who she is.

When He (Jesus) had called the people to Himself, and with His disciples also, He said to them,

> **Whoever desires to come after Me, let him deny himself, and take up his cross, and follow Me. Mark 8:34 NKJV**

Jesus wasn't saying to forsake who He gifted us to be. We are to deny the lustful passions of our flesh, the selfish tendencies to live a "me first" life. We surrender our selfish will to Christ and follow Him into a generous life, a caring, outward focused life. With your priorities in place, your gifts and natural abilities will be elevated and used by God in the ways He designed you to serve.

Nehemiah gave all glory to God. The impossible was accomplished with God's help. This is the key to every talent, skill, gift or natural ability that you have. It is God who equipped you, God who called you, God who sustains you. Work hard, do what you are great at doing, and give Him the glory.

--- the Book of ---

ESTHER

for such

a time as

this

For if you remain

completely silent at this time, relief and deliverance will arise for the Jews from another place, but you and your father's house will perish. Yet who knows whether you have come to the kingdom for such a time as this? Esther 4:14

Esther is the story of the unlikely Queen of Persia, a Jewish orphan, raised by her cousin, whom God used to prevent a disaster. One young woman, her cousin, and the loving providence of God, saved Israel, literally, from total ethnic cleansing.

At the crescendo of the story, Esther must speak to the King, reveal her identity as a Jew and plead for her people. The risk is that the King will reject her and order her to be killed for her deception. Esther devised a plan and entreated Mordecai, her cousin, to quietly call the people to fast and pray for her.

Interestingly, in the Septuagint, the Greek version of the Old Testament, there are more verses than in the more modern translations, including intercessory prayers by Mordecai and Esther. For example, after Mordecai tells Esther what she must do, Esther pleads to God on behalf of the people. It is a beautiful prayer from a desperate heart, during which Esther prays:

> Grant to my mouth proper words in the presence of the lion... Save us by Your hand, and help me who am alone and have no one but You, O Lord. Esther 4:17r-s LXX

God answered her prayer, gave her the plan, gave her mouth the words and saved the people. There are times in life when you will find yourself in a similar situation, not exactly the same as Esther with the lives of a nation in the balance, but times when you're on your own. No one else can step up, or maybe no one else will, or they just don't see the situation the way you do, and you are compelled to speak. God hasn't revealed the gravity of the moment to them. He's chosen you, positioned you. But, you're not alone. God is with you.

With a humble and repentant heart and a will that is surrendered to Christ, He will help you, put the right words in your mouth, lead you to speak before lions, use you to love, serve, heal and restore. Esther stepped up and God saved His children. What if she hadn't?

Well, Mordecai was rightly convinced that God would save them some other way, and He would have. But, God has chosen to work primarily through people, and getting to be a small part of His restoration plan in the lives of others is such a humbling honor that it is hard to imagine wanting to do anything else.

For a moment, consider the implications of Esther's intervention. The book of Esther comes after Nehemiah in the Bible, but the events in Esther happened about 30 years before Nehemiah returned to Jerusalem to rebuild the wall, thirty years before Ezra led the revival in Jerusalem. If Haman had his way and the Jews were annihilated, would there have been anyone with Nehemiah's skills left? Would Ezra have been alive to write it all down?

We believe, like Mordecai, that God would have brought deliverance another way, but the point is that our choices and decisions have implications that will extend far beyond our solitary lives. Things we do affect others for good or for ill.

What, then, is the path of wisdom as you try to do as little harm as possible and as much good as you are able? Jesus said:

> 'You shall love the Lord your God with all your heart, with all your soul, and with all your mind.' This is the first and great commandment. And the second is like it: 'You shall love your neighbor as yourself.' On these two commandments hang all the Law and the

Prophets. Matthew 22:37-40 NKJV

Thus, everything in the Old Testament, the Exodus, the Law, the Promises, and the courage of Esther all comes down to this: love God with your entire being, and love your neighbor as yourself. This will open a door to a life of generosity, self-denial, sacrifice, mercy and love—a Christ-like life.

--- *the Book of* ---

JOB

I know that
my redeemer
lives

For I know

that my Redeemer lives, And He shall stand at last on the earth. Job 19:25 NKJV

The book of Job is probably one of the earliest stories of the Bible. The Septuagint establishes Job as a historical person at the end of chapter 42 where we learn he was in the family line of Abraham, Isaac and Esau. Esau was Job's great-grandfather, and Job lived near the border of Edom and Arabia.

This account isn't fiction. The tragic events described in Job really happened. Like many people, Job's life was blind-sided by tragedy. When calamity happens, it is devastating. The world slams to a stop. Nothing seems important anymore. The pain, grief and loss are overwhelming. We don't know if we can go on. We don't know if we even want to go on.

Some people reading this have been there, or are there now. Job lost his children, his livelihood and his health, all in the blink of an eye and just fell to the ground in shock and grief. As he sat, devastated, in a pile of ash, scraping with broken pottery grievous sores that ravaged his body, people, including his own wife, pleaded with him to just give up—to curse God and die.

Job was a God-fearing man. He believed in God, trusted God and lived a righteous life. His faithfulness was even noted by God. He loved God and was known by God. Not everyone has that kind of faith. Most never even consider a devotion and relationship to God that permeates every aspect of life.

Some people believe in God but live for themselves. Some believe casually, because of their heritage, but their faith is not very personal. But not Job. Throughout the book, Job remains faithful., even though he doesn't understand why everything is happening, and nothing makes sense. All he hears from others is blame and accusation: "It's your fault." "You brought this on yourself." "What did you do? Think back to your childhood." "What sin are you hiding?"

Sadly, some of us have come under similar assault, and sometimes justly because some life choices and behaviors have consequences that come along later and strike us down. But not Job. He had done nothing to bring this calamity upon his life and family. He racked his brain, as we would, but He kept landing in the same place, whatever this was all about, He would simply trust God.

Then, in the middle of the book, when he had reached rock bottom, Job makes a declaration. He wants his friends, his wife, Satan, God and everyone who would ever hear of his story, to know what he really believed after everything was stripped away. This is his core. The essence of his being.

He says:

> Oh, that my words were written! Oh, that they were inscribed in a book! That they were engraved on a rock With an iron pen and lead, forever! For I know that my Redeemer lives, And He shall stand at last on the earth; And after my skin is destroyed, this I know, That in my flesh I shall see God.
> Job 19:23-26 NKJV

In other words, "This is all I know, but I know it for sure! You can carve it on rock with an iron pen forever! I know that my Redeemer lives, and He shall stand at last on the earth, and after this old body is gone, I know one thing, I shall see God."

There is a randomness to life in our fallen world, and there isn't a single person who is exempt from sorrow and pain.

Inexplicably, some will experience extreme pain and devastation. If your life is built on anything other than the solid rock of Jesus Christ, you will crumble under the weight. Because neither your bank account, your family, your looks, your intelligence or anything else you might rely on for security can stand the weight of devastating loss.

The only hope of surviving, making it through, even learning, being healed and ultimately helping others, is the love of God in Jesus Christ.

God's answer to the tragedy and randomness in the world is Jesus.

Through His crucifixion, Jesus took all the world's sufferings upon Himself. He carried the weight for all of human kind. By grace, He now regenerates our nature, changes our perspective, and gives us a foundation, solid and unshakable, upon which to stand in the midst of suffering and declare, "I know that my Redeemer lives! And, after this is over, I shall see God."

- - - *the* B o o k *of* - - -

PSALMS

the language
of the
heart

Let everything

that has breath praise the Lord. Praise the Lord!

Psalm 150:6 NKJV

While it is entirely valid to pray under our breath in our mind and heart, and it is equally valid to "hear" or sense God's "still, quiet voice" in our inner-man, we express ourselves best through our breath. Using words of meaning, sighs of sorrow, cries of heartache or joyful laughter, we communicate thoughts, beliefs, thanks, needs and feelings.

Using words, the Psalms comprise a timeless conversation between God and man, one in which the future is revealed, and history is given context. Through these songs, prayers and poems, we are taught life lessons, obedience and sound doctrine. By example and instruction, we learn how to conquer passions and gain dominion over our soul.

There is something about a song lyric or a story that triggers our mind to store it in an accessible place, somewhere it can be quickly found when needed. An oldie that you haven't heard for years can come on the radio, or an old hymn is turned to in church that you haven't sung since you were a child, and you remember every word, sing along with every note as if you sing it every day. It was stored in your mind, and you didn't even realize it.

This is because songs and stories bypass our mental defense system where our opinions are protected. We all have this brick wall in the front of our mind that somehow vets all the information that comes in through conversation, debate, media reporting and print, quickly scans it for anything that disagrees with what we already believe, and, finding any yellow flags, patently rejects the content.

Songs and stories somehow slip passed this wall, and, as a result, truth can subversively sneak into our hearts undetected, working to change and heal us from the inside out. Jesus always taught with stories for this very reason. Stories are how He conveyed truth to the uninterested. Songs and stories both work this way.

This is why the Psalms are the prayer book and a songbook for ancient Israel and for the church. These words of truth when prayed and sung will slip through the bars of limited understanding, opinions and bias and settle in the mind where they are stored. You might not be able to find them when you want them, but they'll be there when you need them.

The Psalms communicate the condition of our soul at any given time. Whether there is questioning and complaining, or praise, blessing and thanksgiving, the Psalms express the depths of our thoughts and feelings we are unable to articulate. Jesus quoted the Psalms multiple times, even during the anguish of the cross when He cried out the words of Psalm 22, describing that very experience and the hope of salvation He was bringing to the world through His sacrifice.

As you read and sing through the Psalms, Jesus, the Incarnate Word, will teach you how to pray, how to listen, how to live, love and forgive. His Word will be rooted deep in your soul, lead you to a virtuous life, and with your every breath, express the language of the heart and every emotion you will ever feel.

> Oh, the joys of those who do not follow the advice of the wicked, or stand around with sinners, or join in with mockers. But they delight in the law of the Lord, meditating on it day and night.
> Psalm 1:1-2 NLT

PROVERBS

Jesus Christ,
the Wisdom
of God

The fear of the Lord

is the beginning of wisdom, And the knowledge of the Holy One is understanding. Proverbs 9:10 NKJV

Solomon was the principal author of Proverbs, but there was an Author behind the author Who really inspired the book, and that was Jesus Christ.

In writing about learning and knowing Wisdom, Solomon is ultimately pointing forward in time to knowing Jesus— Who is the Wisdom of God.

... Christ the power of God, and the wisdom of God.

1 Corinthians 1:24 NKJV

So in learning the Proverbs, we also learn of Jesus, and our obedience to the instructions in the Proverbs leads to our obedience to Jesus and our openness to be instructed by Him.

Gaining the wisdom of the Proverbs leads to a virtuous life that is emptied of self, and filled with humility, discernment, discipline, astuteness, perception, perspective and so much more. We discover that the fruit of wisdom is, ultimately, the fruit of the Spirit, a humble, selfless, godliness that manifests in our lives as "love, joy, peace, patience, kindness, goodness, faithfulness, gentleness, and self-control." Galatians 5:22-23 NLT

Solomon writes that the journey to wisdom begins with the fear of the Lord.

Much is written about the idea of the fear of the Lord. Some explain the idea in terms of reverence and awe for God's sovereign majesty, His omnipotence and grandeur, and it is certainly that. Others are slow to dismiss the idea that fear means fear, something that frightens you, not a vengeful, "boogieman" kind of fear, but a fear of judgment and the offense of our sinful actions in light of God's holiness.

For many of us, our introduction to Jesus was a combination of these things beginning with whatever our perception of God was at the time. Mixed with that was a sense of fear of judgment and hell, but also, and by far the most compelling part, was the love of God expressed through Jesus.

Learning of His love brings our fear of God into perspective.

Learning that Jesus is God incarnate, and that He left the glory of heaven and became human for the purpose of redeeming humanity and did so with such overwhelmingly selfless love, even when we were still sinners, moves us to love and repentance.

We love Him because He first loved us." 1 John 4:19 NKJV

Fear was the beginning of knowing Jesus, and it led to reverence, understanding and, ultimately, **"to know the love of Christ which passes knowledge; that you may be filled with all the fullness of God." Ephesians 3:19 NKJV**

--- *the Book of* ---

ECCLESIASTES

your own
downward
path

But I did find this:

God created people to be virtuous, but they have each turned to follow their own downward path.

Ecclesiastes 7:29 NLT

Ecclesiastes is a kind of investigational autobiography describing the meaning of life from a human perspective. Solomon deems himself uniquely qualified to teach about meaning since he has achieved everything a human being could possibly desire. Intelligence, wealth, wisdom, authority, power, pleasure—he had it all. So, in an attempt to let people know what lies at the end of the road, he offers the advice of one who has been there and done that.

In the book, he discusses various life paths, including: knowledge, pleasure, wealth, philosophy—literally anything one could desire. And, his conclusion is that life is meaningless. Everything is temporary, fleeting, vain and futile, because every life, rich or poor, slave or free, pauper or prince, ends the same way—in death.

Death is the great equalizer. It's the imposing hurdle that human beings can't jump. From his human perspective, the best he can advise is that one should just enjoy daily life, eat, drink and enjoy work because that is all there is.

It is sad when life is observed to be all there is and after a few fleeting years, you die and cease to exist, everything you did forgotten, everything you had, left behind. You were born with nothing, and you leave with nothing. So what's the point of it all? It's meaningless, or, as Solomon repeats throughout the book, "like chasing the wind."

While the wisdom that Solomon proposes rings true, it is not "The Truth", because the human view is missing the key reality. It doesn't allow for a relational connection to a loving, creator God. The Truth is that God is intimately involved with His creation and has a higher purpose for humanity, a plan full of meaning, value and purpose, revealed in the One Who is Truth, Jesus Christ. This is the exact opposite of the human view of life that Solomon so accurately explains.

Life without hope would be a futile, meaningless waste. But life is never solitary and without hope. God is here, and He is near to every person who desires more than the downward path they are currently traveling.

He has put eternity in their hearts... Ecclesiastes 3:11 NKJV

Inherent in every life from conception is the God-placed knowledge that this life is not all there is. It is pushed far to the back of many lives through hardship, struggle, pain or success and victory, but it is there nonetheless. Many times this still, small voice, this knowledge of something or someone more, pushes to the front of our consciousness during times of failure or rejection.

For some, it is a revelation. For others, just a glimpse, but they realize in that moment that God is real and that He loves them.

For Solomon, who did know these things but was disciplined in writing these thoughts from the vantage point of human achievement, he closes the book with an admonition to young people about their walk with God.

Young people, it's wonderful to be young! Enjoy every minute of it. Do everything you want to do; take it all in. But remember that you must give an account to God for everything you do.
Ecclesiastes 11:9 NLT

So live life, take it all in, but don't forget God in the process.

Don't let the excitement of youth cause you to forget your Creator. Honor him in your youth before you grow old and say, 'life is not pleasant anymore.' Ecclesiastes 12:1 NLT

In other words, honor God when you are young, because this is when your life truly finds its center, its core. Then, when you are old, you will be established in God. This is the only cure for the vanity of life.

That's the whole story. Here now is my final conclusion: Fear God and obey his commands, for this is everyone's duty. God will judge us for everything we do, including every secret thing, whether good or bad. Ecclesiastes 12:13-14 NLT

Jesus said, "If you love me obey my commandments." John 14:15 NLT

Solomon had everything we could imagine life offers, yet something better is available to every person, and that is knowing God. This is the seed planted in every human heart, the one that blossoms when we turn to Jesus and obey His commands, the one that will turn the downward path of our own selfishness into a fulfilling, abundant and eternal life.

SONG OF SOLOMON

the Love Story of Christ and the Church

I am my beloved's

and my beloved is mine… Song of Solomon 6:3a NKJV

Song of Solomon is the perfect book to follow Ecclesiastes in order. In Ecclesiastes, Solomon looked at life from an earthly point of view and decided, after pursuing every indulgence to the extreme, that life was meaningless vanity.

In the Song of Solomon, however, Solomon again looks at life, but this time from the heavenly perspective of the love of God, and in doing so, gives us an allegorical glimpse into the love of Christ and His Church.

In fact, while the earthly life portrayed in Ecclesiastes is seen as the vanity of vanities, the heavenly view of God's love story is shown as the song of songs—the song above all songs.

Many Jewish teachers viewed the Song of Songs as a symbolic relationship between God and His people until the day of the coming Messiah. Early church fathers interpreted the book as an allegory of the relationship between Christ and the Church. Neither group necessarily saw the Song of Solomon as a literal story of Solomon's marriage to a beautiful Jewish peasant girl, which the story loosely suggests in its "Cinderella" type narrative . But, certainly, as a story, it is a compelling and vivid tale!

A young girl looks up one day to see a handsome stranger, a shepherd, who looks intently at her and tells her, **"You are altogether beautiful, my love. There is no flaw in you." Song of Solomon 4:7 ESV.**

The two draw close to one another and fall in love. But, time passes in a blur, and he leaves, promising first that he would return. She believes him.

Her time is spent thinking only of Him, remembering their love, their time together, longing for his return. She describes him to her friends in intimate detail and can't stop thinking about him day and night.

Then, one day there is a commotion in the village, and everyone stops to see the carriage of the king approaching with a full security detail! The King summons her and she soon discovers that her shepherd love is, in fact, the King. He sweeps her away to the palace where they can love each other for all time.

The church is the young girl, and Jesus is the King who comes in the form of a shepherd, the Good Shepherd. After giving Himself freely, demonstrating His consummate love, He went away, promising to return one day. And, the church longs for Him, talks about Him, thinks about Him all the time. And one day He will return and sweep us away to a marriage feast like no other in heavenly glory. How beautifully this reflects the love of God through Jesus Christ.

In Revelation, Apostle John writes of his vision of heaven, given by Jesus. John bore witness to the very event Solomon had written about under the inspiration of the Holy Spirit, the wedding feast of Christ and the Church.

> Then, I, John, saw the holy city, New Jerusalem, coming down out of heaven from God, prepared as a bride adorned for her husband"
> Revelation 21:2 NKJV
>
> Alleluia! For the Lord God Omnipotent reigns! Let us be glad and rejoice and give Him glory, for the marriage of the Lamb has come, and His wife has made herself ready. And to her it was granted to be arrayed in fine linen… Revelation 19:6-8 NKJV

In Song of Solomon, we journey heavenward for a glimpse of what John would one day see, and we learn of the unwavering, unfailing, eternal love of God for His children, the church. In the end, we are left to say to anyone who does not yet know His love, Come, experience the love of the shepherd King for yourself. Life for you doesn't have to be in vain; you can know the Song of Songs.

--- *the* Book *of* ---

ISAIAH

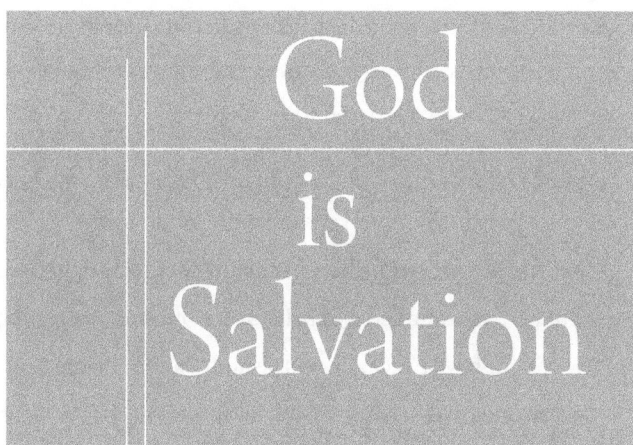

God
is
Salvation

In all their suffering

he also suffered, and he personally rescued them In his love and mercy he redeemed them. He lifted them up and carried them through all the years. Isaiah 63:9 NLT

One day in my late teens I was sitting on a bench at a college campus, reading Isaiah 53 and was just overwhelmed at the detail of Isaiah's prophecy and felt like I had to share it with someone. I'm sure you have had moments like this when you discovered something that struck you as genuinely amazing. Another young man was studying at the other end of the bench, and I looked over and said, "Excuse me, can I read you something?"

He looked up and kind of refocused himself, seeing that I was just a regular student-type like him, "Sure, I guess," he said. And, I read:

Yet it was our grief he bore, our sorrows that weighed him down. But he was wounded and bruised for our sins. He was beaten that we might have peace; he was lashed—and we were healed! We— every one of us—have strayed away like sheep! We, who left God's paths to follow our own. Yet God laid on him the guilt and sins of every one of us!

He was oppressed and he was afflicted, yet he never said a word. He was brought as a lamb to the slaughter; and as a sheep before her shearers is dumb, so he stood silent before the ones condemning him. From prison and trial they led him away to his death. But who among the people of that day realized it was their sins that he was dying for—that he was suffering their punishment? He was buried like a criminal, but in a rich man's grave; but he had done no wrong

and had never spoken an evil word. Isaiah 53:4-9 TLB

I got about that far and looked up. He was still with me. I asked him, "Do you have any idea who that is talking about?"

And he said, "It's talking about Jesus, clearly."

I said, "Are you a Christian?"

"No, but, I mean, that's talking about Jesus, right?" he said.

I said, "Yes, but this is blowing me away."

"Why? Aren't you a Christian? I mean, you're sitting there reading a Bible," he said incredulously.

I said, "Yes, but this was written over seven hundred years before Jesus was even born. It sounds like it was written by someone who watched it happen."

"Seven hundred years?" he said.

"Yeah," I said. He just shook his head and looked down at my Bible. He was without words.

I never asked the guy if he wanted to become a Christian or ever saw him again for that matter, but the look on his face betrayed his heart. Isaiah had got him thinking.

Isaiah spoke of the future as if it were the past. So exact and specific were his prophecies that, even in his lifetime, they seemed completely impossible. Isaiah spoke of Cyrus the King of Persia by name 100 years before the gentile ruler was even born. And he described the exact actions Cyrus would take to restore the Jewish nation to their homeland—before they had even been exiled. And, during Isaiah's life, and continuing after his death, the word of the Lord spoken by him came to pass exactly as he had spoken.

Isaiah was truly the mouthpiece of God during a profoundly difficult time in Israel's history. The nation would be divided into northern and southern king-doms during his lifetime, as brother turned against brother and tribe against tribe. God used Isaiah to warn of the judgment they were bringing upon themselves, explaining the cost of their disobedience, the loss of land and life, but, for the most part, the people didn't listen.

However, woven throughout the book are promises that reached far into the future, prophetic messages from God about a Messiah, a Deliverer of God's people, not from Pharaoh or Babylon this time, but an ultimate deliverance from sin and evil.

He begins with the promise of how Christ would come; He would be born of a virgin.

Therefore the Lord Himself will give you a sign: Behold, the virgin shall conceive and bear a Son, and shall call His name Immanuel. Isaiah 7:14 NKJV.

Immanuel, that is, "God with us." The promised one would be God Himself, conceived by the Holy Spirit and born of the virgin, Mary, thus to have a dual nature, divine and human. This was the only way salvation could be accomplished.

The Law not only revealed our sinfulness, it revealed our helplessness to overcome the sinfulness. We needed God's help. We needed Him, personally, and He would come. He promised it through Isaiah (and others). He promised to come Himself.

> **In all their suffering he also suffered, And he personally rescued them In his love and mercy he redeemed them. He lifted them up and carried them through all the years. Isaiah 63:9 NLV**

Dear one, God knows you can't redeem yourself, but you're not the first one to try. Salvation is something He had to do for you—for us. God is salvation. Surrender, and trust Him today.

--- *the* Book *of* ---

JEREMIAH

sometimes things

get worse before

they get better

See, I have this day

set you over the nations and over the kingdoms, To root out and to pull down, To destroy and to throw down, To build and to plant.
Jeremiah 1:10 NKJV

Jeremiah was called to be a spokesperson for God early in life. The personal and beautiful way God speaks to Jeremiah reminds us again of the sanctity of life and God's love and involvement in a life from the moment of conception.

Before I formed you in the womb I knew you; Before you were born I sanctified you; I ordained you a prophet to the nations
Jeremiah 1:5 NKJV

With God there are no "fetuses", there is no discussion of "viability." There are children, people He knows and loves and sets apart for special relationships with Him in life.

Then said I: "Ah, Lord God! Behold, I cannot speak, for I am a youth." But the Lord said to me: "Do not say, 'I am a youth,' For you shall go to all to whom I send you, And whatever I command you, you shall speak. Do not be afraid of their faces, For I am with you to deliver you," says the Lord. Jeremiah 1:6-8 NKJV

Jeremiah set out from there with messages for kings, leaders and nations, messages that came directly from God, and he was soundly rejected at every turn. Jeremiah's life was kind of like a nightmare where you have a message that can save the world from some catastrophe, and you run through the streets shouting, and people can see you, but they can't hear you. You get right in their face and yell, and they just look at you with a blank stare, and then everyone is surprised when calamity comes because they weren't expecting it.

Only in Jeremiah's case, they could hear his warnings about Babylon and how they were coming to destroy Jerusalem, but he was a lonely voice as there were plenty of false prophets who said the opposite. But instead of just ignoring Jeremiah, they beat him, imprisoned him, lowered him into a well to sink in a quagmire of gooey mud and die (he didn't). He is known as the weeping prophet because of the heartbreak he experienced as people ignored his impassioned message.

It seems that when the end is truly near, the deception of the enemy, the weight of darkness, can lead normally rational people to believe, even practice, the most irrational, horrible things. In Judah, instead of turning to God for relief from the famine, poverty and disease, people began doing unmentionable evil including sacrificing their children to the false god, Molech, which is not unlike the modern world aborting children for selfishness and convenience.

And then, just as was foretold, Judah was overthrown, many people died, and others were taken captive to Babylon. The city and beloved temple were destroyed, and Jeremiah, the weeping prophet, continued pleading for people to repent.

In the midst of bleakness and despair, God spoke to Jeremiah and revealed His plan, a New Covenant. Out of the rubble, when the time was right, God was going to create a New Covenant with mankind. He said:

> Behold, the days are coming, says the Lord, when I will make a new covenant with the house of Israel and with the house of Judah... I will put My law in their minds, and write it on their hearts; and I will be their God, and they shall be My people... for they all shall know Me... For I will forgive their iniquity, and their sin I will remember no more. Jeremiah 31:31-34 NKJV

The New Covenant is going to be personal, not juridical, for, somehow, God is going to step in and fix the brokenness of the relationship between God and man that has plagued mankind since the Garden of Eden.

He gave Isaiah a glimpse into the New Covenant when He showed Isaiah the suffering servant, the Messiah, who would die for the sins of the world. The New Covenant would be Jesus! It would not be a document written on tablets of stone, but, instead, God's Love, His Word, His Son, written on the tablets of the heart. And everyone, Jew and Gentile, would be invited into this covenant.

Jeremiah 31 is quoted in the New Testament book of Hebrews in speaking of Jesus, where the writer concludes:

> For by the power of the eternal Spirit, Christ offered himself to God as a perfect sacrifice for our sins. That is why he is the one who mediates a new covenant between God and people, so that all who are called can receive the eternal inheritance God has promised them. For Christ died to set them free from the penalty of the sins they had committed under that first covenant. Hebrews 9:14-15 NLT

Jeremiah was the prophet for God in a day much like today, when stubborn, selfish people were all going their own way without regard for God. Judgment came. Today, God has made a New Covenant with mankind through Jesus Christ. He has already taken upon Himself the penalty for your sins and mine, His part of the covenant is settled. But, we must do our part. We must enter into covenant with Him by faith in His finished work.

So, this, then, is the basis of all judgement, Christ's life, death and resurrection. Receive your eternal inheritance and freedom from the penalty of sins through Christ and Christ alone.

--- *the Book of* ---

LAMENTATIONS

songs from
rock
bottom

Joy has left our hearts;

our dancing has turned to mourning. The garlands have fallen from our heads. Weep for us because we have sinned. Our hearts are sick and weary, and our eyes grow dim with tears. For Jerusalem is empty and desolate, a place haunted by jackals. Lamentations 5:15-18 NLT

Lamentations is a collection of five songs of mourning and loss, written by Jeremiah shortly after the siege of Babylon and the destruction of Jerusalem. The Babylonians had come in hard, just as Jeremiah and other prophets had been warning the people of Judah for decades, and, in their wake, they left total devastation. People were either killed, tortured, carried away to Babylon or left to starve in the desolate rubble. Children were orphaned, fainting and dying in the streets. Others perished in their mother's arms.

There was no water, no food, no temple, no wall of protection. In what seemed like an instant, the once great City of David, the lavish palace and temple of Solomon, the welcoming place to kings and nations, the Promised Land of Abraham, Isaac and Jacob, destroyed, the people scattered, killed, rounded up as slaves. It had never been this bad, and it couldn't get any worse. Judgment had come.

This was rock bottom, and it could have been avoided. This is what broke Jeremiah's heart. This is what breaks the heart of people today who see the world sliding toward the same end. We know better!

Do not be deceived, God is not mocked; for whatever a man sows, this he will also reap Galatians 6:7 NKJV

For they sow the wind, and they reap the whirlwind... Hosea 8:7 NKJV

Behold, the Lord's hand is not shortened, That it cannot save; Nor His ear heavy, That it cannot hear. But your iniquities have separated you from your God; And your sins have hidden His face from you, So that He will not hear. Isaiah 59:1-2

Please also see Romans 1:18-32. The righteous judgment of God, His wrath against ungodliness and unrighteousness, extends from His Holiness. He cannot abide sin; it causes His face to be hidden. As Jeremiah writes:

You have hidden yourself in a cloud, our prayers cannot reach you. Lamentations 3:44 NLT

While the Lord is infinitely patient with mankind, sustaining the world and literally holding everything together by the victory of Jesus Christ, Lamentations shows what happens when God lifts His hand, and people receive the true fruit of their unrighteousness and sin. In a word, horror.

Do you wonder how Jeremiah kept his sanity as he saw it coming, then he saw it happen? He hoped in the Lord. He held desperately to what He knew of God's character and love. Jeremiah said:

I will never forget this awful time, as I grieve over my loss. Yet I still dare to hope when I remember this: The faithful love of the Lord never ends! His mercies never cease. Great is his faithfulness; his mercies begin afresh each morning. I say to myself, "The Lord is my inheritance; therefore, I will hope in him!" Lamentations 3:20-23 NLT

In the world today,, there are mothers and fathers, monks and pastors, children and teens, policemen and politicians, world leaders and waiters. People, who, like Jeremiah, have a heart for God and who know the path of self destruction our country and much of the world is on. Like Jeremiah, we must weep, not for ourselves, but for the world.

And, we must stand up with broken hearts and tear-filled eyes, declaring, "Enough is enough! We must turn to God before we are nothing but an afterthought, a punchline, before God wipes us away like one wipes a dish!"

Jeremiah closes the book with a plea that should be echoing today from every church and every Christian home, every session of Congress and every bedside prayer time:

> **Restore us, O Lord, and bring us back to you again! Give us back the joys we once had! Lamentations 5:21 NLT**

--- the Book of ---

EZEKIEL

it takes all kinds

But look,

I have made you as obstinate and hard-hearted as they are. I have made your forehead as hard as the hardest rock! So don't be afraid of them or fear their angry looks, even though they are rebels. Then he added, Son of man, let all my words sink deep into your own heart first. Listen to them carefully for yourself... Ezekiel 3:8-10 NLT

While Jeremiah stayed in what was left of Jerusalem, Ezekiel, Daniel and others were taken to Babylon. Ezekiel was God's prophet there in Babylon, but his message wasn't for the foreigners. It was for his own people who still hadn't learned anything even though they had lost everything.

Ezekiel was a unique character, seemingly part priest, part thespian. Ezekiel often employed physical demonstration to drive the message of God home to the people. He once laid on his left side for 390 days, representing Israel's rebellion, and then turned onto his right side for another 40 days to represent Judah's sin, all the while tied up and unable to roll from one side to the other.

God gave Ezekiel fantastic visions and messages to declare, most of which went unheeded by his fellow exiles. God told him to speak them anyway and he did, because God knew Ezekiel was the kind of man who would do anything. Ezekiel was obstinate and hard-headed. In fact, God said Ezekiel's head was as hard as a rock.

Know anybody like that? Most of us do. Some parents and teachers are frustrated with obstinate or hard-headed children, but God has wired them this way for special assignment. And, as He gave Ezekiel his unique calling, He revealed the key to directing the hard-headed life. God says:

...let all My words sink deep into your own heart first. Listen to them carefully for yourself. Ezekiel 3:10 NLT

Then go... Deep, careful, personal knowledge of God's word, carefully applied to their own life first, will help obstinate persons stay on the right path.

Some children may, like Ezekiel, have a head like a rock, but if their heart is steeped in God's word, they will likely be fine. Ezekiel was unique—one of a kind. Just like every child of God, there are no two alike. You don't have to fit into a certain mold to know God and be known of Him. You just have to believe and be available. And, to those who seek Him, He will always be found by them.

In fact, even though the children of Israel would be scattered among the nations after Jerusalem was destroyed, the place they called home occupied by foreigners and their house of worship reduced to rubble, God did not leave them, not a single person, from the time they were scattered until the time He began bringing them back home.

God said:

... Although I have cast them far off among the Gentiles, and although I have scattered them among the countries, yet I shall be a little sanctuary for them in the countries where they have gone. Ezekiel 11:16 NKJV

God promised that He, Himself would be their haven, safe place or little sanctuary. No matter where they went, no matter who else they might be with, no matter how they might be treated or whether they were accepted and loved, rejected and ignored, God would be there for them.

What a wonderful promise to all of us this is, but especially to anyone who feels just outside the mainstream. You can know that God is outside the mainstream as well, and right there with you.

God is our refuge and strength, always ready to help in times of trouble. Psalm 46:1 NLT

There is nothing to fear. He knows your quirks and your weaknesses, and He is there for you. He is your safe place. Jesus said, **"If anyone loves Me, he will keep my word; and My Father will love him, and We will come to him and make Our home with him." John 14:23 NKJV**

God loves each of His unique and peculiar people, dear one, and He makes His home, a little sanctuary, with each of us who love Him and keep His word.

--- *the* Book *of* ---

DANIEL

God
is in
charge

Daniel

Blessed be the name

of God forever and ever, For wisdom and might are His. And He
changes the times and the seasons; He removes kings and raises up
kings; He gives wisdom to the wise and knowledge to those who
have understanding. He reveals deep and secret things; He knows
what is in the darkness, And light dwells with Him. Daniel 2:20-22
NKJV

Daniel was a contemporary of Ezekiel and Jeremiah. Like Ezekiel, Daniel was
among the people exiled to Babylon from Jerusalem after Judah was overthrown and demolished. The Book of Daniel is full of amazing stories that ig-
nite the imaginations of children: Daniel in the lion's den, who was sovereignly
protected by God, and Shadrach, Meshach and Abednego, the faithful Hebrew
men who would not bow to a false idol. These three were thrown into a blazing
furnace of fire so hot that it killed people outside the furnace with its intense
heat. Yet, the three young men remained alive in the midst of the furnace, as
cool and fresh as a dewy spring morning, protected by the Lord, who joined
them in the furnace. These stories and more are found in the exciting book of
Daniel!

It is a book of apocalyptic detail which has animated eager Bible students
desiring to decipher Daniel's imagery and assign the fantastic passages to
current and future events. When we read Daniel, we tend to think of the future
because of how he alludes to it, which is understandable and even intended by
God.

But, also, think of the context. Daniel is in a foreign land with the opportunity
to speak to Kings and Rulers about the wonderful works of God. Through fasting, prayer, an amazing grasp of the Law, history and a whole-hearted devotion

to God, Daniel speaks about the sovereign God to the unbelieving Gentile rulers of the known world! One after another, these pagan dictators are left to admit the authority and power of God. Now, it typically drives them mad, but they have to admit that there is a power higher than the King, and He is God Almighty!

Daniel is like the Christians today who selflessly seek the Lord through prayer, fasting and study. These people see the "big picture" regarding world events. They are not shaken by anything in the news, because in everything, they know something is going on behind the scenes that the cameras never catch. God is at work. It's the difference between walking in darkness and walking in light. Jesus said,

> I am the light of the world. He who follows Me shall not walk in darkness, but have the light of life. John 8:12 NKJV

While people of the world are walking around in darkness, falsely perceiving their importance, behaving selfishly, seeking to build little personal kingdoms, God's people have a different perspective. They see all this leading somewhere. They are not shortsighted. They know that God is watching, and Jesus is coming soon. They know that good times are the blessing and beauty of God, and difficult times are for pruning and purging. Everything we go through is a time for repentant hearts and greater dependence on the Lord Jesus.

In the Septuagint version of Daniel, there are extra verses at the end of chapter 12 and another story. In this story, we see Daniel laughing at the folly of those trying to trick the king into worshipping false gods. He laughs because it is ludicrous. As serious as this life can be, sometimes people are just idiots, and it is just impossible not to shake your head and laugh at the folly of the world.

Really, though, it's not funny. The deprivation and sin of the world is horribly real, so be vigilant, be watchful, follow Jesus' lead, and shine on.

--- the Book of ---

HOSEA

Gods unfailing love

Then the Lord

said to me, "Go again, love a woman who is loved by a lover and is committing adultery, just like the love of the Lord for the children of Israel, who look to other gods and love the raisin cakes of the pagans." Hosea 3:1 NKJV

God called Hosea to be a prophet to the northern tribes of Israel after the kingdom had divided, with the ten tribes of Israel to the north and the tribes of Judah and Benjamin in the south. During this tumultuous time in history, there were other prophets including Amos in the north and Isaiah and Micah in the south. Through these holy men, God spoke to the wayward children of Israel and the revolving door of Kings.

Hosea is the strangest, most improbable, love story in the Bible. Similar to Ezekiel, God called Hosea to personally demonstrate what God was saying to the people. But whereas Ezekiel had an almost theatrical oddness in his prophecy, Hosea was asked to do something common, but do it in an unexpected way. God asked Hosea to get married.

We thank God that monogamous, heterosexual—marriage is still something our generation can relate to. But, with the cultural acceptance, even expectation, of sex outside of marriage, it gets harder by the day to maintain biblical values and, as a result, understand the incredible thing God asked Hosea to do.

He was told to marry a prostitute, which he did, a young Israelite named Gomer. Now, that's not so strange in itself because people fall in love, and everyone has a past. One of the beautiful miracles of marriage is that the union itself will sanctify the couple through lives of faithfulness to one another. But, that's not what happened.

Some time after giving birth to several children, Gomer left and returned to her former life. The very idea that a spouse would abandon her family for other lovers, even prostitution, would crush the faithful partner and likely damage the children immeasurably. And, we know that it happens every day in the modern world because of sexual addiction, gender confusion and, really, basic selfishness. Of course, in the current climate, such behavior is understood based on the apparent mitigating circumstances of neglect, abuse, unhappiness or some other contributing factor. However, in the case of Hosea and Gomer, it is understood to be a completely one-sided breakup.

Curiously though, God told Hosea to go and find his wife, rescue her from her sordid life and restore her to himself in love. Hosea did that, literally, purchasing her freedom as one would buy a bag of beans.

That would be a difficult proposition for a modern man or woman. Pride, trust, love, respect—everything that was held between the couple, forfeited by selfishness, now forgiven, forgotten, as the offending party is sought out, pursued and bought back. That would be hard. God used this extreme example not necessarily to show us how we should be, although this is true, unfailing love. But, more so, it shows how God's love is different. It is higher and deeper than we could ever imagine.

He is, specifically, showing Israel that after they discover the emptiness of living alone, serving fleshly gods that only take and use. He would be there for them. He would pursue them and stay close and draw them back to himself. He would pay whatever price was required for their redemption. And, He did. Through Jesus Christ the Father redeemed mankind, He bought back a bride out of prostitution.

But God demonstrates His own love toward us, in that while we were still sinners, Christ died for us. Romans 5:8 NKJV

And, He changes us. We are no longer what we were, we are sanctified, and made new.

> I will betroth you to Me forever; Yes, I will betroth you to Me In
> righteousness and justice, In lovingkindness and mercy; I will
> betroth you to Me in faithfulness, And you shall know the Lord.
> Hosea 2:19-20 NKJV

The betrothed would be a virgin, and when we are redeemed, God restores our virginity regarding all our sin. In other words, we are cleansed and made truly new!

We are washed by the blood of the Lamb! We all know how hard it is to change our ways, to truly repent from prostituting ourselves to sin. We all know people who seem so far gone they could never be redeemed, even if they wanted to be. We can even become weary in praying for them as we see them get worse instead of better. But that is the wonderful thing about God's unfailing love, because while He waits for us to turn, He promises to help us return to Him, even in our weakness!

> ... The Lord is His memorable name. So you, by the help of your
> God, return; Observe mercy and justice, And wait on your God
> continually. Hosea 12:5-6 NKJV

Keep praying for the Gomers in your life, dear one. They will know who to call when everything falls apart. His name is memorable, and He promises to help them return. Hallelujah!

--- *the* Book *of* ---

JOEL

here
is the
plan

Joel

Tell your children

about it in the years to come, and let your children tell their children. Pass the story down from generation to generation. Joel 1:3 NLT

Not much is known about the prophet Joel. His little book, on the other hand, has been very well known over the centuries. For one reason, the first thing God said to Joel was to tell children about it, and pass it down from generation to generation.

This is clear when, on Pentecost, some 700-900 years later, the Apostle Peter instantly recognizes what is happening there in Jerusalem when God, the Holy Spirit, visited Christ's followers in a powerful display. He declared to the gathering crowds, "This is what Joel was talking about!" Not only Peter, but that great throng of Israelites from all over the known world, were familiar with Joel. They knew the story.

It is the story of God's plan for the ages, revealing the future of the world.

Joel begins with the worst natural disaster people of his day could have imagined. A plague of locusts would come and ravage the landscape, leaving nothing edible in their wake. Then another swarm would follow the first one, and then another and another. Four consecutive hoards would march, unstoppable, through the land and literally rape and lay bare the entire landscape, leaving people devastated and without hope.

Events like these, tornados, earthquakes, hurricanes, you can't plan for them; you have to be ready. And, not just physically, you have to be prepared spiritually, or you will be left with despair and hopelessness.

Joel calls people to repentance and tells them of the love and mercy of God.

Turn to me now, while there is time. Give me your hearts. Come with fasting, weeping, and mourning. Don't tear your clothing in your grief, but tear your hearts instead. Return to the Lord your God, for he is merciful and compassionate, slow to get angry and filled with unfailing love... Joel 2:12-13 NLT

This has always been God's call. This is your only life. Don't waste it on vain pursuits. Sin will ultimately leave you empty. Instead, repent, give God your heart, enter the joy of His salvation and know the One True God.

Then Joel cracks open an unexpected window to describe a time when God, the Holy Spirit, would enter the lives of God's people. People of Joel's day were familiar with God anointing kings, priests and prophets, like Joel, with His Spirit— but everyone? Even children? Gentiles? Joel writes,

Then... I will pour out my Spirit upon all people. Your sons and daughters will prophesy. Your old men will dream dreams, and your young men will see visions. In those days I will pour out my Spirit even on servants—men and women alike. Joel 2:28-29 NLT

Several hundred years later, Peter and the other followers of Christ experienced this very event on Pentecost following Christ's resurrection and ascension. Jesus told them to wait in Jerusalem until they received the promised Holy Spirit Who would baptize them, empowering them to be Christ's witnesses to the world.

Subsequently, Joel notes that "everyone who calls on the name of the Lord will be saved." Joel 2:32 NLT.

The victory of Christ's resurrection and the outpouring of His Spirit on all flesh brought together Jew and Gentile, repairing the breach and making all one in Christ.

ACTS

the
early
church

In my first book

I told you, Theophilus, about everything Jesus began to do and teach... Acts 1:1 NLT

The physician Luke wrote both the Gospel of Luke and the Book of Acts, addressing both to a person named Theophilus. Theophilus, which means "one who loves God," was most likely an actual person, especially as Luke adds, "most excellent" which might suggest that Theophilus was possibly a ranking official or officer. But, in a general sense, Theophilus could be all of us who love God and yearn to know the stories of Jesus and the early church.

Interestingly, Luke opens Acts by telling Theophilus that his first book, the Gospel of Luke, contained *"everything Jesus began to do and teach."* The inference, then, is that Acts contains the things Jesus continues to do and teach.

Historically, Tiberius was the Roman leader when Jesus was crucified. He was succeeded by Caligula, so the events described in Acts occurred generally during the time of Caligula, Claudius and Nero, who killed himself just a couple years before Jerusalem was leveled by Titus in 70 A.D. The fact that Christianity spread and flourished under the often times brutal persecution of Rome is a testimony, first, to the fact that God's will for the Church is supernatural and cannot be quenched by evil men. Secondly, it is a testimony to the personal grit and sense of mission of the Christians.

Christ and His Kingdom wasn't just something they believed in; it was something they staked their lives on. They knew Jesus was Lord. He met them, changed them, gave them purpose. Satan thinks about Christians the same way he thought about Job, when he said to God, in essence, just put a little pressure on, and he will fold like a bath towel.

But, he couldn't be more wrong.

Jesus said, "But you will receive power when the Holy Spirit comes upon you. And you will be my witnesses, telling people about me everywhere—in Jerusalem, throughout Judea, in Samaria, and to the ends of the earth." Acts 1:8 NLT

The power of the Holy Spirit at work in the Body of Christ is an unstoppable, unbeatable force that the very gates of hell cannot prevail against.

In the book of Acts, just as today, persecution against Christians will most often backfire, as the persecutors are met with love and forgiveness, and the masses see the difference between the people following the doctrine of Jesus and the senseless meanness of their persecutors.

The Book of Acts didn't end with the last period in chapter 28. We are left there with the Apostle Paul under house arrest in Rome, waiting for an audience with Caesar. Jesus' work didn't stop there, nor has it stopped today. Jesus is still God Incarnate (in human form), but now, sitting at the right hand of the Father, everliving to make intercession for us, He is incarnate through His Body, the Church.

We are Christ's hands and feet, sharing the Good News of the Gospel to the people of our generation. Through good times and bad, come what may, Christ is still on the throne, and our mission is to share His redeeming love with a broken and hurting world.

His love will prevail today, through the acts and actions of your life, as it did through Paul, Barnabas, Peter, Stephen and the other saints and heroes of the early church. What will your chapter say? I have a feeling, it will be good!

--- *the Book of* ---

ROMANS

being truly human

Sin is no longer

your master, for you no longer live under the requirements of the law. Instead, you live under the freedom of God's grace. Romans 6:14 NLT

Prior to his miraculous conversion to Christ, Saul of Tarsus was a highly educated Pharisee, a firebrand of Judaism who volunteered to travel the countryside rounding up and jailing followers of Jesus for their apostasy.

We see Saul first in the book of Acts as he stands supervising the stoning of the mighty Christian deacon, Stephen, who unapologetically directed his accusers to Christ Jesus, the promised Messiah. After the stoning of Stephen, Saul began persecuting Christ's followers in earnest. It was during one of these posse-like excursions that Jesus got ahold of Saul and confirmed what Stephen and others had been declaring.

Saul, knowing the Old Testament and the Law more than most, by the revelation of God, instantly knew everything he'd heard about Jesus was true and real. Simultaneously, he realized he was a deeply sinful and deceived man. He thought himself to be pleasing to God for his loyalty to his training in the Law of Moses —when he was actually fighting against God the whole time. All this came rushing into his psyche and he just asked, **"Lord, what do You want me to do?" Acts 9:6 NKJV**

God gave Saul instructions and when Ananias, the man God called to go to Saul, prayed for him, literal scales fell from his eyes. The physical blindness he'd experienced since meeting the Lord on the road was healed, but more importantly, the spiritual blindness he hadn't even known was there was removed and, for the first time, he could truly see.

After several years of traveling, preaching and fleeing attempts on his life, Saul, now using his Roman name, Paul, began writing letters to places he had visited and established followers of Christ including Galatia, Thessalonica and Corinth among the first. Then, perhaps compelled by his calling as apostle to the Gentiles, Paul wrote his first letter to a city he had not yet visited, Rome, the cultural center of the Roman Empire.

Romans is different than the other letters. Here, more than in any of his writings, Paul writes about being human, more specifically, the experience of life with and without God's grace. Through the course of the letter, he weaves a literary tapestry by contrasting and comparing life with and without Christ, as both Jewish and a Roman citizen, carnal and spiritual. He is able to speak with authority about the lives most have, and, conversely, the life everyone could have.

So now there is no condemnation for those who belong to Christ Jesus. And because you belong to him, the power of the life-giving Spirit has freed you from the power of sin that leads to death. The law of Moses was unable to save us because of the weakness of our sinful nature. So God did what the law could not do. He sent his own Son in a body like the bodies we sinners have. And in that body God declared an end to sin's control over us by giving his Son as a sacrifice for our sins. He did this so that the just requirement of the law would be fully satisfied for us, who no longer follow our sinful nature but instead follow the Spirit.

Those who are dominated by the sinful nature think about sinful things, but those who are controlled by the Holy Spirit think about things that please the Spirit. So letting your sinful nature control your mind leads to death. But letting the Spirit control your mind

leads to life and peace. For the sinful nature is always hostile to God. It never did obey God's laws, and it never will. That's why those who are still under the control of their sinful nature can never please God. But you are not controlled by your sinful nature. You are controlled by the Spirit if you have the Spirit of God living in you. (And remember that those who do not have the Spirit of Christ living in them do not belong to him at all.)
Romans 8:1-9 NLT

Paul who in one place referred to himself as the **"chief of sinners"**(1 Timothy 1:15) knows better than most how the sinful nature can keep even the most religious person separated from God. Saying the right words, fasting, even being zealous for everything you think is right, is of no value from a selfish and sinful heart. Paul has learned, and calls us, to cultivate a different life, a Spirit-controlled life.

Dear one, God did for you what you could never do on your own, through Christ, God declared an end to sin's control over you. Surrender afresh to the Holy Spirit's control, leading you to peace with God and abundant life in Christ, in spite of any physical circumstances. This is being fully human. This is the life of grace.

--- *the Book of* ---
I CORINTHIANS

love, the

more excellent

way

And now abide

faith, hope, love, these three; but the greatest of these is love. 1
Corinthians 13:13 NKJV

Paul may have intended on a brief stay in Corinth, stopping at the Grecian port
city on his way home from Athens, but God had other plans. It was in Corinth
that he met Aquila and Priscilla, transplants from Rome who also happened
to be tentmakers like Paul. He stayed with them and worked while preaching
to Jews and Greeks in the Synagogue. God gave Paul a vision to speak boldly
in Corinth and he did, with many people being baptized into Christ including
the ruler of the local synagogue. Paul stayed there for a year and a half estab-
lishing a local church. This was in 51 A.D.

A few years after he left, word had gotten back to the apostle that there were
some problems in the young church. Paul wrote them a lengthy letter of cor-
rection. He spoke to each issue with apostolic authority, while reminding them
of spiritual realities and a more excellent way to live.

Reading about the problems in the Corinthian church is kind of like seeing a
car pulled over for speeding. As we drive past, we realize almost all of us were
doing the same thing, but this guy got caught.

This letter could have been written in any of the last twenty centuries to just
about any group of people who organized under the banner of a church. How
can I be so sure? Because there are people involved.

And people are predictable.

People tend to follow the big names. "I follow Paul." "I follow Apollos." We do
the same thing. If a certain speaker says it, it's gospel, profound, revelatory. We'd
follow them off a cliff, which is where following a man (or woman) often leads.

True leaders, like Paul and Apollos, are fellow servants of Christ. They're not trying to gain followers for themselves, they're gathering others to stand with them before the King of Kings.

People practice and/or condone immorality. The word used for fornication in 5:1 is *"porneia,"* does that sound familiar? And Paul says such a one should be put out of the church until the lusts of the flesh are burned up. Pornography, fantasy, fornication, adultery, secrecy, sex before and outside of marriage— these practices and addictions are crushing souls and ruining lives. Contemporary culture may be the worst of all time. But, Paul's word is simple when it comes to sexual immorality— Run!

> Run from sexual sin! No other sin so clearly affects the body as this one does. For sexual immorality is a sin against your own body. Don't you realize that your body is the temple of the Holy Spirit, who lives in you and was given to you by God? You do not belong to yourself, for God bought you with a high price. So you must honor God with your body. 1 Corinthians 6:18-20 NLT

People are full of pride and arrogance. Many gifted brothers and sisters in the Corinthian church seemed to be bickering selfishly about sharing their spiritual gifts in the assembly.

I think of the body-building competitions sometimes featured on television when I was a child. In these contests six or eight huge, musclebound men, would smile and pose for applause and notice, jockeying for position, nudging one another aside, preening for the judges. It was quite a spectacle. I'm not making a direct comparison. The simple point is that a worship service is not a talent competition, not a body-building contest.

The church is not a contest to see who is smarter, more inclusive, more doctrinally sound or who has a better design aesthetic. This is the church:

God is faithful, by whom you were called into the fellowship of His Son, Jesus Christ our Lord. 1 Corinthians 1:9 NKJV

The church is people, imperfect, ordinary people who have been called out of the world by our faithful God, called out of the selfish behavior of the world and into a fellowship. We are called into fellowship with Jesus Christ, literally, kinship or communion with Christ, walking in His steps, selfless, humble, preferring others, sharing generously.

Dear one, don't be burdened by worldly vices that want to follow you into communion with Christ. Leave those bags at the door of repentance. Enter to love the Lord Jesus, to be changed by Him and to love your neighbor with unconditional love.

Be on guard. Stand firm in the faith. Be courageous. Be strong. And do everything with love. 1 Corinthians 16:13-14 NLT

--- *the* B o o k *of* ---

2 CORINTHIANS

a more
excellent way
of life

For our boasting

is this: the testimony of our conscience that we conducted ourselves in the world in simplicity and godly sincerity, not with fleshly wisdom but by the grace of God, and more abundantly toward you. 2 Corinthians 1:12 NKJV

Apostle Paul most likely wrote his second letter to the church in Corinth not too long after the first letter. First Corinthians is corrective and instructional, directing the church to leave worldly vices behind. The selfishness of the old life has no place in their new life and certainly not in the Body of Christ. Then, he compels them to learn to walk in love, the more excellent way.

In the second letter, Paul writes about what walking in love looks like, what the Corinthians could look forward to in the more excellent way of life in Christ.

Self-proclaimed ministers arose behind Paul. With suspect credentials, they arrogantly twisted and distorted Paul's words, setting themselves up as authorities, super apostles, who knew much better than Paul, whom they discounted as a side-show wannabe. They spoke ill of Paul's troubles, the persecution, the unending hardships, even his speech and general persona.

You know how it feels to be talked about behind your back. Most of us have experienced someone putting us down in order to elevate themselves. What do you do? Get in their face and tell them to back down and get their facts straight? Shame them back on social media? Defend yourself by showing the flaws in their thinking? Or, just keep quiet, and trust the Lord to defend you. This is hard; it is real life.

Paul would have been justified in any of a number of responses to the accusers, but he reacted differently than expected. He didn't take the bait. He responded, not in fleshly wisdom, but by the grace of God. (1:12).

Instead of traveling back to Corinth and confronting these men, Paul wrote another letter, this time showing how the things they accused him of were, actually just further proof of the goodness of God and the power of Jesus resurrection.

> Not that we are sufficient of ourselves to think of anything as being
> from ourselves, but our sufficiency is from God, who also made us
> sufficient as ministers of the new covenant...
> 2 Corinthians 3:5-6 NKJV
> For we do not preach ourselves, but Christ Jesus the Lord, and
> ourselves your bondservants for Jesus' sake. For it is the God who
> commanded light to shine out of darkness, who has shone in our
> hearts to give the light of the knowledge of the glory of God in the
> face of Jesus Christ. 2 Corinthians 4:5-6 NKJV

Paul stressed sincerity and simplicity, sharing the truth of Jesus Christ from a selfless, humble heart, focusing always on our Savior, Jesus, consistently pointing people to Him, no matter how they felt about Paul as the messenger. His only worry was that the Christians would believe the nonsense of his accusers.

> I fear, lest somehow, as the serpent deceived Eve by his craftiness,
> so your minds may be corrupted from the simplicity that is in
> Christ. 2 Corinthians 11:3 NKJV

Satan will twist and distort the simplicity of the message of the cross. He'll do so through men and women who feign depth and intelligence and posture themselves over others. With no standard of interpretation or accountability, people can preach whatever they want.

> For if he who comes preaches another Jesus whom we have not
> preached, or if you receive a different spirit which you have not

received, or a different gospel which you have not accepted...

2 Corinthians 11:4a NKJV

A different Jesus, a different spirit, a different gospel... and Paul's greatest fear for his dear Christian friends, was that—

...you may well put up with it! 2 Corinthians 11:4b NKJV

Sometimes people will tolerate a different gospel, a different spirit, even a different Jesus, if the message otherwise appeals to some other selfish appetite. Don't be deceived away from the simplicity of Christ. Love is the more excellent way. Here is how that love manifested itself in the life of the apostle Paul.

We give no offense in anything, that our ministry may not be blamed. But in all things we commend ourselves as ministers of God: in much patience, in tribulations, in needs, in distresses, in stripes, in imprisonments, in tumults, in labors, in sleeplessness, in fastings; by purity, by knowledge, by longsuffering, by kindness, by the Holy Spirit, by sincere love, by the word of truth, by the power of God, by the armor of righteousness on the right hand and on the left, by honor and dishonor, by evil report and good report; as deceivers, and yet true; as unknown, and yet well known; as dying, and behold we live; as chastened, and yet not killed; as sorrowful, yet always rejoicing; as poor, yet making many rich; as having nothing, and yet possessing all things. 2 Corinthians 6:3-10 NKJV

In many believers around the globe this is love unveiled through life. For the underground Christians in Asia, for the hunted believers in Ethiopia and Sudan. Christianity isn't a promise of health and wealth in this life. It is the promise of communion with Jesus Christ, and the joy of seeing other people, and the very fabric of society, changed by His radical goodness.

--- *the Book of* ---

GALATIANS

faith
working through
love

Stand fast therefore

in the liberty by which Christ has made us free, and do not be
entangled again with a yoke of bondage.

Galatians 5:1 NKJV

The area of Galatia, now modern Turkey, was home to several communities of
Christians that Paul had established, and was comprised of both Gentile and
Jewish converts. As was the case in most of the places he traveled, it was just a
matter of time before the know-it-alls, called Judaizers, attempted to add their
spin to what Paul had taught.

They challenged Paul's credentials, his authority and his message, and, in
many cases, attacked him personally as he presented an easy target. It appears
there are always people who will buy the latest fad and the Judaizers found an
audience in Galatia.

The problem of these false teachers, though, was that Paul hadn't made up his
message out of the clear blue sky. It **"came through the revelation of Jesus
Christ"** (Galatians 1:12 NKJV). And Paul had been commissioned, personally, to preach the message by **"Jesus Christ and God the Father who raised
Him from the dead."** (Galatians 1:1 NKJV). So, guess who is going to win
this debate? Paul's teaching came from Christ Himself.

The Judaizers wanted to steer the Christian faith, which had necessarily come
through the Jewish religion, back to the traditional practices of keeping the
Law. It made sense to them that if Christianity was a product of Judaism, then
the Christians should be first Jewish, then Christian. So the Gentiles would
need to be circumcised, keep the commandments, attend synagogue, observe
the feasts and the whole deal— and, of course, the Jewish converts would
"simply" return or remain in legalistic obedience to their tradition. It seemed

like a good idea to them...

But, it was not a good idea. This wasn't just a stricter version of Christianity. What they were proposing was a different gospel, a false, perverted gospel meant to please men and, ultimately, shift power to themselves.

Paul saw this as a defining moment for the faith and drew a hard line in the sand. He reminded the Galatians that right standing with God and justification comes by faith in Christ Jesus, not by obedience to the Law.

> Yet we know that a person is made right with God by faith in Jesus Christ, not by obeying the law. And we have believed in Christ Jesus, so that we might be made right with God because of our faith in Christ, not because we have obeyed the law. For no one will ever be made right with God by obeying the law. Galatians 2:16 NLT
> Let me put it another way. The law was our guardian until Christ came; it protected us until we could be made right with God through faith. Galatians 3:24 NLT

Paul describes the place of the law in history and religion and explains how the doctrine of Jesus is the new way, it is the New Covenant. Christianity was birthed from Judaism, but it is for the whole world, not just one group of people. It is a New Covenant based on God's unmerited favor bestowed on all humanity through the victory of God the Son, Jesus Christ, conquering sin, death and the grave. This is where faith has found its resting place.

> Stand fast therefore in the liberty by which Christ has made us free, and do not be entangled again with a yoke of bondage. Indeed I, Paul, say to you that if you become circumcised, Christ will profit you nothing. And I testify again to every man who becomes circumcised that he is a debtor to keep the whole law. You have

become estranged from Christ, you who attempt to be justified by law; you have fallen from grace. For we through the Spirit eagerly wait for the hope of righteousness by faith. For in Christ Jesus neither circumcision nor uncircumcision avails anything, but faith working through love. Galatians 5:1-6 NKJV

Religion can be like a forced, lifeless, bondage—a burden that we carry out of guilt or tradition, trying to measure up to standards that better people than us have failed at living.

We may be free from the Judaizers that pestered the Apostle Paul and the Galatians, but how many of us have been told about all the things we do that we shouldn't do, or need to do but don't do? "God would heal you if you'd stop fill in the blank." So you try, and you fail, and you feel guilty and worthless, and you're met with a shrug and raised eyebrows because you are hurting and it's your own fault— Bondage!

Doing everything right won't work, not that we could, anyway. If we are in bondage to religious duty, trying to coerce the hand of God, **"Christ will profit you nothing... you will become estranged from Christ."** (5:1-6). Why? Because we're trying to be justified by something other than His grace—actually, we fall from grace! Religious activity can't save us—the only thing that matters is faith working through love; that's it. In practice, dear one, our lives should be full of good deeds, things done to bless and heal others in loving action., not for our salvation, but because of it. It is faith working through love.

I have been crucified with Christ; it is no longer I who live, but Christ lives in me; and the life which I now live in the flesh I live by faith in the Son of God, who loved me and gave Himself for me. Galatians 2:20 NKJV

--- *the Book of* ---

EPHESIANS

the mystery
of
His will

...having made known

to us the mystery of His will, according to His good pleasure which
He purposed in Himself.

Ephesians 1:9 NKJV

The people of Ephesus were dear to the Apostle Paul. He spent a lot of time
there, at one point basically renting a room and teaching for over two years.
People came and went, and the good news of Jesus was spread throughout
Asia Minor. In fact, back in Acts chapter nineteen, Luke writes that during this
time, **"All who dwelt in Asia heard the word of the Lord Jesus, both
Jews, and Greeks." Acts 19:10 NKJV**

Later, while traveling through the area, Paul called for the Ephesian elders to
meet with him, and he spoke very personally to them, warning them of false
teachers who would come, and sharing with them they likely wouldn't see
him again. They prayed and wept, expressing their love for one another (Acts
20:17-38).

Then, when Paul was in Rome under house arrest, he wrote this letter to his
dear friends in Ephesus. In the letter to the Ephesians, Paul systematically
answered the BIG question, the mystery, what everyone wanted, and still in
this day, wants to know. It is a question that comes in many forms, "Why am I
here?" "What is truth?" "Is there a God?" "What is the meaning of life?" "What
is God's will?"

Have you ever whispered something like this in the quietness of your room or
maybe shouted at the top of your lungs when everything seemed to be going
against you? Sure, because sometimes we feel desperate and need to hold on
to. something. We cry out with one question leading to another, and it always
comes down to this, "What is God's will?"

The one answer to all of life's biggest questions was formulated in the mind of God before the foundation of the world. Then, year after year, and generation after generation, His plan was put in place, and the very history of the world began moving toward this revelation. Prophets hinted at it. Historical events symbolized it. And, in the fullness of time, God unveiled it.

The mystery of God's will, in a word, is Jesus.

Jesus Christ, God the Son, God incarnate, Emmanuel, is Lord and Messiah. By His life, sacrificial death, burial and resurrection, He has once and for all conquered sin and death, restoring what was forfeited by the original humans— restoring the life of the world. Everything in creation that was lost to sin, now redeemed and made new.

Christ removed the distinctions between people and restored the community of mankind in the Church, His body. For in Christ, all are one, a tapestry of brilliant color encompassing the world. Jesus hinted at the mystery when He told his disciples, **"At that day you will know that I am in My Father, and you in Me, and I in you." John 14:20 NKJV**

Jesus will dwell in an individual person by the presence of God the Holy Spirit in their heart, and that person, along with all followers of Christ, will, in turn, dwell in Christ. Spiritually, our lives are **"hidden with Christ in God,"** (Colossians 3:3). And, physically, we are each a part of His Body, dwelling by faith in the mystical, universal, yet local and identifiable, Body of Christ—the Church, an organism that transcends language and border, making all people one in Christ.

There is a debate in modern culture as to whether the local church is important anymore, if it is relevant. Technology has made all the "services" of the church, like teaching, preaching and worship, available with the tap of a smartphone screen. Why drive across town and "attend" one more function? We are so busy, after all.

But, notice, the church isn't an assortment of spiritual services you can take or leave. The church is something else entirely and part of the mystery of Christ. Those buildings are just gathering places. If anything, they probably work to separate us more than bring us together. Where God is truly building something is among us, in our midst, both locally and globally.

> **In whom the whole building, being fitted together, grows into a holy temple in the Lord, in whom you also are being built together for a dwelling place of God in the Spirit. Ephesians 2:21-22 NKJV**

God is building a dwelling place for Himself, not in a building made of stone or by hands, but in a gathering of people, redeemed and clothed in the righteousness of Christ.

Think for a moment about heaven. What do you imagine it will be like? Living in the presence and loving mercy of God Almighty, the victorious Jesus, God the Son, and God the Holy Spirit, the Spirit of Life and Truth. Will there be strife? Will there be division? Will children go unwanted, unloved or abused? Will widows go without? Will young people be abandoned? No, no, no, no and no. In heaven no one will be left behind, for all are loved, and all are one.

This is what God is doing here on earth, now. This is the Mystery of His will, the Kingdom of God—on earth as it is in heaven.

Dear one, Jesus is the answer. We are living in the culmination of society and culture. These are the days when God is moving in power through His dwelling place in the Spirit—the Church. Don't be a spectator, don't be a loner. Open your eyes and your heart and watch as God reveals the mystery of His will in our generation. There is a special place reserved for you to be part of the miracle. Step in.

--- *the Book of* ---

PHILIPPIANS

life

together

...fulfill my joy

by being like-minded, having the same love, being of one accord, of one mind. Philippians 2:2 NKJV

The Church in Philippi had an unusual beginning which we find in Acts chapter sixteen. It seems Paul was headed to Asia when the Holy Spirit somehow prevented him. Then, Paul had a vision of a man from Macedonia, a region in Southern Europe, calling to Paul to come and help them. Paul left immediately, changing course and subsequently introducing the life-changing message of Jesus to the influential city Philippi and all of Europe.

In those days, Philippi was like a miniature Rome with ornate, imposing architecture, opulent living and not a large religious presence. Paul and his cohort located a place by the riverside where locals gathered for prayer, and they went there to tell people about Jesus. A certain woman named Lydia heard their testimony and believed. She and her household were baptized and invited the disciples to her home.

Later, Paul and the brothers with him were arrested for the bogus charge of disturbing the peace, and they were beaten with rods and tossed in jail, secured with stocks and chains like hardened criminals.

As the story goes, they were singing and praising God late into the night when a great earthquake rocked the prison, and all the prisoner's chains were loosed, and cells were opened. The jailer, realizing the situation, considered suicide rather than facing the implications of all the prisoners escaping through the night. But, Paul called to him from the dungeon and said, "Hey, don't worry, we're all here." The jailer ran down with a light and found all the prisoners there with Paul. The jailer was moved to repentance, believing in Jesus Christ, the power of God, and he was baptized, and his whole household were baptized.

Such were the beginnings of the first church in Europe, the Church in Philippi. From two families, Philippi would become instrumental in Paul's ministry and among Christian groups they didn't even know personally, as they gave generously from what God supplied, whether a little or a lot.

This is what we learn from Philippians, that the Christian life should never be reduced to a personal belief system. More rightly, Christianity is a shared dynamic—a communion of life, relationship, selfless service and generosity.

> for your fellowship in the gospel from the first day until now, being confident of this very thing, that He who has begun a good work in you will complete it until the day of Jesus Christ;
>
> Philippians 1:5-6 NKJV

God's work is both individual and corporate. The good work He is doing is in our midst, in the body. It is this work that He is going to complete. But, it is possible only when individuals deny themselves and serve in simplicity and humility.

> Fulfill my joy by being like-minded, having the same love, being of one accord, of one mind. Let nothing be done through selfish ambition or conceit, but in lowliness of mind let each esteem others better than himself. Let each of you look out not only for his own interests, but also for the interests of others.
>
> Philippians 2:2-4 NKJV

Our society is cocooning more than ever. Like countless little caterpillars, we busy ourselves spinning sealed-off lives that are seemingly self-sufficient. And, the more self reliant we become, the more security we convince ourselves that we have. But, our little silken fortresses aren't nearly as impregnable as we think. Without people, a community or tribe, without family or trusted friends, without a like-minded community of believers who will drop everything and come to you—and, at the same time know you would do the same for them—our actual security is imagined at best.

Consider your life. What would happen if, like Job, you lost everything, your job, your cell phone, your internet, your home, your family, your health? If you walk down that path very far you realize that our lives are extremely fragile, and a belonging community of Christ is the best and really, only, safeguard against total destitution.

Then, consider the millions of people around the world who are already there. They've lost or never had any of the things we take for granted and just exist from day to day without hope. They don't have a safety net. Think of the broken families, single parents and orphaned, vulnerable children, trying to cope with impossible circumstances, people with disabilities, the hurting and hungry right outside our doors. Who will help them?

Dear one, the message of Philippians is that joy in life, true fulfillment, comes to us through selfless generosity, unity, humility and living life together. Try, today, to see the world through different eyes, then, ask the Lord to let you see the world through His eyes.

Let this mind be in you which was also in Christ Jesus...
Philippians 2:5 NKJV

--- *the Book of* ---

COLOSSIANS

no more

high-sounding

nonsense

Don't let anyone

capture you with empty philosophies and high-sounding nonsense
that come from human thinking and from the spiritual powers of
this world, rather than from Christ.

Colossians 2:8 NLT

The young Colossian church was being infiltrated by false teachers who
seemed to be adding to the simplicity of the Gospel. Nothing wound the clock
of the Apostle Paul more than people who felt compelled to customize or
complicate the Good News of Jesus.

The teaching was called gnosticism, which had the general idea that Jesus had
revealed some inside scoop to a few men, some behind-the-scenes spiritual
hokus pokus that would elevate a person's Christian experience. The root
of gnostic is "gnosis," meaning knowledge. They flaunted deeper insight and
knowledge. This "knowledgeism" appeals to our basic desire both to be right
and to know something others don't. But, it is false, wrong-headed knowledge.
Having a lot of spiritual sounding, wrong information is still wrong, no matter
how much of it you have.

The Gospel of Jesus Christ is as deep as any knowledge a person could ever
attain, but it is, at the same time, so simple and easy to understand that it is
accessible to all. Paul fought to keep it that way, telling the Colossians,

> Don't let anyone capture you with empty philosophies and
> high-sounding nonsense that come from human thinking...
> Colossians 2:8 NLT.

So, Paul reminds the brothers and sisters of Colosse about the basics of their
faith, the absolutes, the truth of Christ Jesus that wasn't up for debate because it
was the revelation and Word of God. He used an old song they may have sang

at their baptism or in fellowship with other believers. Rich with the doctrine of Christ, His Incarnation, His Deity and His Lordship and redemption on the cross, Paul writes;

> Christ is the visible image of the invisible God.
>
> He existed before anything was created and is supreme over all creation, for through him God created everything in the heavenly realms and on earth.
>
> He made the things we can see and the things we can't see—
>
> such as thrones, kingdoms, rulers, and authorities in the unseen world.
>
> Everything was created through him and for him.
>
> He existed before anything else, and he holds all creation together.
>
> Christ is also the head of the church, which is his body.
>
> He is the beginning, supreme over all who rise from the dead.
>
> So he is first in everything.
>
> For God in all his fullness was pleased to live in Christ, and through him God reconciled everything to himself.
>
> He made peace with everything in heaven and on earth
>
> by means of Christ's blood on the cross.
>
> Colossians 1:15-20 NLT

Jesus Christ is God incarnate, Emmanuel. He is the mystery of God, the secret plan, Christ Himself. **In Him lay all the treasures of wisdom and knowledge** (see 2:2-3), and, on top of all this, **He lives in you** (1:27). Paul encourages the Colossians to live in the simplicity and freedom of this truth, cultivating their life with Jesus.

> ...continue to follow him. Let your roots grow down into him, and let your lives be built on him. Then your faith will grow strong in

the truth you were taught, and you will overflow with thankfulness.
Colossians 2:6-7 NLT

Through our baptism we died to our old life and were raised to new life with Christ (3:1). In turn, "put to death the sinful, earthly things lurking within you" (3:5 NLT), "... now is the time to get rid of anger, rage, malicious behavior, slander and dirty language. Don't lie to each other, for you have stripped off your old sinful nature and all its wicked deeds." (3:8-9 NLT) "Christ is all that matters, and he lives in all of us." (3:10 NLT).

This is what it's all about, the simplicity of Christ. The beautiful truth that by His immeasurable grace He changes us into the best version of ourselves and fills us with unspeakable joy through life.

"Let the message about Christ, in all its richness, fill your lives..." (3:16 NLT) And, "Above all, clothe yourselves with love, which binds us all together in perfect harmony" (3:14 NLT).

Keep life simple. No more high-sounding nonsense.

--- *the Book of* ---

I THESSALONIANS

encourage

each other with

these words

And now,

dear brothers and sisters, we want you to know what will happen to the believers who have died so you will not grieve like people who have no hope. 1 Thessalonians 4:13 NLT

Paul established the Thessalonian church on his second missionary journey and wrote this letter a short time afterward, making it one of the earliest New Testament books, penned only twenty years or so after Christ's resurrection and ascension to heaven. Paul was only in Thessalonica for about three weeks. In that time, he led many people to faith in the Lord Jesus Christ, from Jewish people who heard him preach in the synagogue, to God-fearing Greeks, and many prominent women.

The Jews who didn't believe, however, were offended by Paul's message and came at him with force, gathering a mob and dragging some of the new believers to court. Paul and Silas had to escape the city by night. These angry Jews from Thessalonica followed them, causing trouble and forcing Paul's group to keep moving. Their charge against Paul was interesting. They declared, **"Those who have turned the world upside down have come here too!"** Acts 17:6 NKJV

This was how the Jewish non-believers in this metropolitan city in Greece perceived Christians, just twenty or so years after Jesus' resurrection—that they had turned the world upside down.

Long ago, in the Garden of Eden, the perfect world flipped because of the bad choices of the original humans. Death and selfishness would reign on earth in place of life and goodness. This was the opposite of God's intent. It was upside down. And, after two thousand years, people had gotten used to living upside down. It's what they knew. Selfishness, pride, self-preservation, that's humanity.

Then Jesus came, and, in the view of most of the religious crowd, turned the world upside down. His incarnation, death, burial and resurrection had set everything on its head. And they were offended—and still are. But for those who look closely, we see that Jesus actually restored the original design. He renewed human goodness, destiny and purpose. He restored life and defeated death.

Dear one, the world is never really going to understand why you are different. People tilt their head and try to see, but to them, right-side up will always look upside down.

There was so much about the young church that was going well, and that they were doing right, so Paul encouraged them to stay strong in the faith, and he prayed that their love would continue to grow and overflow (1 Thessalonians 3:5,12). And, he teaches that God's will, in the simplest of terms, is to live holy lives.

> God's will is for you to be holy, so stay away from all sexual sin.
> I Thessalonians 4:3 NLT

> God has called us to live holy lives, not impure lives.
> I Thessalonians 4:7 NLT

Holiness, being separate from the ways of the world and set apart to live selflessly and simply, is God's will for His children.

One of the truths Paul wanted to clarify for the young church was the reality of Christ's return. It was a primary topic of discussion because of persecution and just a general sense of longing and love. It is the same today. Most of we believers have had days when we have longed for Jesus to come back. When a loved one dies, when life is hard, when Jesus is the only one who understands what you're going through. "Oh, Lord Jesus," we pray, "come back soon." Paul didn't discourage their longing; he just clarified it for them.

What if a Christian dies before Christ returns? When will Jesus return and how should we prepare? So Paul assures them:

> And now, dear brothers and sisters, we want you to know what will happen to the believers who have died so you will not grieve like people who have no hope. For since we believe that Jesus died and was raised to life again, we also believe that when Jesus returns, God will bring back with him the believers who have died.
> I Thessalonians 4:13-14 NLT

> We tell you this directly from the Lord: We who are still living when the Lord returns will not meet him ahead of those who have died. For the Lord himself will come down from heaven with a commanding shout, with the voice of the archangel, and with the trumpet call of God. First, the believers who have died will rise from their graves. Then, together with them, we who are still alive and remain on the earth will be caught up in the clouds to meet the Lord in the air. Then we will be with the Lord forever. So encourage each other with these words. I Thessalonians 4:15-18 NLT

Don't worry so much about when He will come, just know that He will. For Paul assures the church that the important thing is that we walk in the light, clearheaded, protected by faith and love, confident in His gracious salvation.

> So encourage each other and build each other up, just as you are already doing. I Thessalonians 5:11 NLT

--- *the Book of* ---

2 THESSALONIANS

patient

endurance

May the Lord

lead your hearts into a full understanding and expression of the love of God and the patient endurance that comes from Christ. 2 Thessalonians 3:5 NLT

Communication is interesting. You can control what you say, but you cannot control what people hear. You can choose the words you write, but there is no guarantee that they will be understood the way you intended. This is the challenge of good communication. Many times we just hear what we want to hear.

This was the case with Paul's communication with the young church in Thessalonica. From the moment the church began, there had been harsh community backlash. While many believed the Word of the Lord, many others did not. As is always the case, the antagonists, without the peace and love of God in their hearts, were vocal and aggressive. Instead of simply coexisting, they somehow feel the need to persecute— and they did.

Paul had taught the young believers that Jesus was coming back. Jesus had promised the disciples on many occasions that His departure was temporary, and that He would surely return for them. God the Holy Spirit, present in their lives since the first Pentecost after Christ's resurrection, would be the guarantee of His certain return. So, it makes perfect sense that these brothers and sisters, just a few weeks old in the Lord, persecuted for their faith from day one, would start talking about the second coming of Jesus. "He's been gone over twenty years, surely He is coming soon."

So, Paul's first letter addressed Jesus' return. He told them in essence that the day of Christ's coming was not something you could find on a calendar. It was information known only to God. But, even so, a date didn't really matter, because whether a person was living or dead at the time of His return, He was returning for all of His faithful ones. The living will gather to Him, and the dead will be raised. Everyone will be together. He told them to encourage each other with those words, (1 Thessalonians 4:13-18).

Then he gave the example of a thief and how he strikes when no one is expecting it, when everyone is asleep. But, again, they didn't have to worry about this because they were children of the Light, children of the Day, they were fully expectant of the coming of the Lord, so it would be a welcome, wonderful event, not a surprise.

Some of the well-intentioned believers there in Thessalonica read Paul's first letter and decided they would not be caught sleeping, so they quit their jobs and spent day and night waiting for the Lord's return. Others became discouraged because Jesus was taking so long, while some began to think He had already come, and somehow they missed it. They had misunderstood parts of Paul's first letter. You can control what you say, but you can't control what people hear.

So Paul writes them again, a letter of deep love and clarification. He confirmed the one thing they had gotten right—Jesus is coming back to earth. Paul added that before the Lord comes, a few things would happen, including a great falling away from the faith, and the antichrist arising and deceiving many. But Paul assures the believers even these facts shouldn't affect their day-to-day lives. God has all that covered.

He's still working His plan, making people whole through the compelling love of Christ and the power of the resurrection. We are part of His plan, His instruments of love and mercy in the world.

Opposition is actually part of our ongoing pruning, helping our faithfulness and endurance, helping our love to grow.

Your faith is flourishing and your love for one another is growing. We

proudly tell God's other churches about your endurance and faithfulness
in all the persecutions and hardships you are suffering. And God will
use this persecution to show his justice and to make you worthy of his
Kingdom, for which you are suffering. 2 Thessalonians 1:3-5 NLT

By the grace of God, our lives will be different, honoring Christ, living by faith,
accomplishing good things for God that the Spirit leads us or prompts us to
do.

So we keep on praying for you, asking our God to enable you to
live a life worthy of his call. May he give you the power to accomplish all the good things your faith prompts you to do. Then the
name of our Lord Jesus will be honored because of the way you
live, and you will be honored along with him. This is all made possible because of the grace of our God and Lord, Jesus Christ.
2 Thessalonians 1:11-12 NLT

In a sense, persecution is like a strong wind in our face, its gusts striking us, trying to knock us off balance, make us fall or turn and run with the wind instead
of against it.

Paul knows from personal experience that living against the wind is hard and
writes:

With all these things in mind, dear brothers and sisters, stand firm
and keep a strong grip on the teaching we passed on to you both in
person and by letter. 2 Thessalonians 2:15 NLT

The second coming of Christ is imminent, dear one. Jesus is coming back. It
is as certain as anything true in the world because God has revealed it in His
Word through Christ Jesus and the Holy Prophets and Apostles. It may be
soon, as each generation is given an expectant spirit because of our love for

Jesus, and it may still be a long way off, as God desires that each person, in every generation, have an opportunity to know His love and be made whole in Christ. Our role is to stand firm on the solid rock of Jesus Christ, to keep a firm grip on the doctrine of Jesus and to live with patient endurance, growing always in love and good deeds.

- - - *the* B o o k *of* - - -

I TIMOTHY

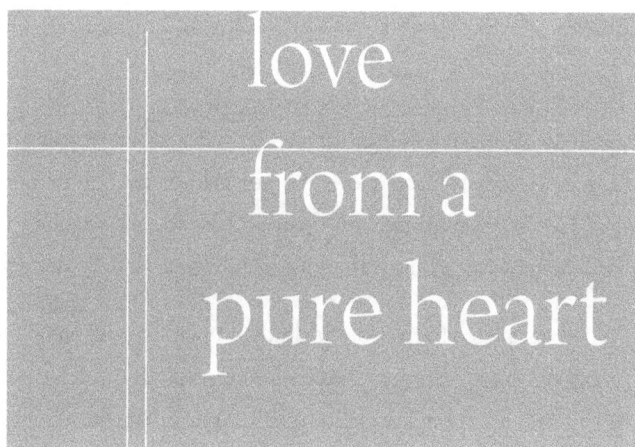

love
from a
pure heart

The purpose

of my instruction is that all believers would be filled with love that comes from a pure heart, a clear conscience, and genuine faith. 1 Timothy 1:5 NLT

Paul had left Timothy in Ephesus to curb the voices of false teachers that were springing up from within the church and without. In doing so, the apostle began to create some structure for the young churches, especially regarding the character of the leaders and their priorities in serving.

Paul's goal for the churches, what he called "the purpose" of his instruction (1 Timothy 1:5), is that each Christian be filled with love.

Love is a natural by-product of knowing God, and being created in His image. The very essence of God is love, and we can love God only because He first loved us. So being created in the image of God means, inherently, being created as loving beings. Love is the core of humanity.

When sin entered the world, and death through sin, this loving core that is the image of God became tarnished. Selfishness and survival take the lead very early in life. But the image of God is still there, you can see it in a babies' eyes, the light, the joy, the love for their mothers, the wonder of discovery.

Children have exactly what Paul said is the whole purpose of his teaching: they are full of love which comes from "a pure heart, a clear conscience, and genuine faith"(1 Timothy 1:5). And, they didn't learn it; it is built in to their humanity.

Jesus said that it is exactly this childlikeness that identifies each person in the Kingdom of Heaven.

But Jesus said, "Let the children come to me. Don't stop them!

> For the Kingdom of Heaven belongs to those who are like these
> children. Matthew 19:14 NLT

He was very literally talking about real children because, when He said this to
His disciples, there were actual toddlers and children clamoring for His attention, and He loved it. The little ones display what Jesus desires in all of us.

We might be surprised on the Day of the Lord to see the number of little ones,
the weak and simple, people who didn't have a voice in this world or who
didn't make it very long for whatever reason, leading the rest of us to the heart
of God. Isaiah's prophecy notes that the little ones will lead the wild animals, so
you never know.

> In that day the wolf and the lamb will live together; the leopard will
> lie down with the baby goat. The calf and the yearling will be safe
> with the lion, and a little child will lead them all. Isaiah 11:6 NLT

Timothy had traveled with Paul, being sent a variety of places with great
responsibility, or left behind with important, foundational precepts to teach
or set in place. Paul trusted him like no other. He was probably, at the same
time, not one who necessarily looked the part or was comfortable with being
in leadership. It seems as though he was very shy, possibly sickly or prone
to weakness, and Paul advised him to take care of himself physically and to
remember that God had given him spiritual gifts to offset what he perceived he
lacked to do his job well.

Paul didn't tell Timothy to "look for people just like yourself," but maybe he
could have. For Timothy, even though he was younger than the others, seemed
to be leading the church, not because of talent, skill or education, but because
of his conduct and character, the things that really matter.

Dear one, I imagine that, like Paul, you sometimes consider yourself "the chief
of sinners" (1:15 NKJV), I sure do. And we feel like the purity of a child, the

love, pure heart, clear conscience and genuine faith, we see in little ones has long passed us by. Our hearts are well-intentioned, but they are also scarred and pitted, with little crevices of darkness that harbor vice and missteps of which we are not so proud.

First, repent from the leftover junk in your life and receive God's mercy.

> **But God had mercy on me so that Christ Jesus could use me as a prime example of his great patience with even the worst sinners. Then others will realize that they, too, can believe in him and receive eternal life. 1 Timothy 1:16 NLT**

Give Him honor and glory for doing in you what you could never do on your own.

> **All honor and glory to God forever and ever! He is the eternal King, the unseen one who never dies; he alone is God. Amen. 1 Timothy 1:17 NLT**

May your life be filled with love from a pure, childlike heart, in Jesus' Name and for His glory.

2 TIMOTHY

living

tradition

Teach these truths

to other trustworthy people who will be able to pass them on to
others. 2 Timothy 2:2 NLT

The second letter to Timothy was quite possibly the last letter written by the
great Apostle Paul. He had a sense that his time was short. He had no hope of
release, and his friends were slowly fading away to do other things. He longed
to see Timothy again, so he wrote this very personal letter asking him to come
as soon as he was able. Paul was martyred under Emperor Nero in A.D. 67.

Think about it: Paul could have written to one or more of the surviving apostles, his peers and the leaders of the Church. Or, possibly Linus, mentioned at
the end of the letter, who would become the next Bishop of Rome, succeeding
Peter and Paul. He could have written to a best friend, a confidant, even a
relative, an aunt or a parent. But he didn't. He wrote to the next generation, to
Timothy, his *"son in the faith"* (1 Corinthians 4:17 NKJV).

This is the miracle of Living Tradition. Jesus taught Paul who poured his life
into Timothy, who, in turn, was instructed to do the same with others.

1. Guard the Truth—by the power of the Holy Spirit, carefully guard the
precious truth.

> Hold on to the pattern of wholesome teaching you learned from
> me—a pattern shaped by the faith and love that you have in Christ
> Jesus. Through the power of the Holy Spirit who lives within us,
> carefully guard the precious truth that has been entrusted to you.
> 2 Timothy 1:13-14 NLT

2. Pass it on—Teach these truths to other trustworthy people who will do
the same.

You have heard me teach things that have been confirmed by many reliable witnesses. Now teach these truths to other trustworthy people who will be able to pass them on to others. 2 Timothy 2:2 NLT

3. Focus on Jesus—Center your life and teaching on the simplicity of Jesus Christ, His death, burial and resurrection, and the faithfulness of God. Explain the Good News clearly, laced with love.

Always remember that Jesus Christ, a descendant of King David, was raised from the dead. This is the Good News I preach.

2 Timothy 2:8 NLT

This is a trustworthy saying:

If we die with him, we will also live with him.

If we endure hardship, we will reign with him.

If we deny him, he will deny us.

If we are unfaithful, he remains faithful, for he cannot deny who he is. Remind everyone about these things, and command them in God's presence to stop fighting over words. Such arguments are useless, and they can ruin those who hear them.

2 Timothy 2:11-14 NLT

4. Be Faithful to the Word—Remain faithful to the holy scriptures, they provide the wisdom to receive salvation.

All Scripture is inspired by God and is useful to teach us what is true and to make us realize what is wrong in our lives. It corrects us when we are wrong and teaches us to do what is right."

2 Timothy 3:16 NLT

Paul trusted that the Apostle's teaching (which would become the New

Testament), plus the Old Testament, along with the inspiration and guidance of God the Holy Spirit, would be enough to keep the Church on track—and, of course, it was.

However, Paul's charge to Timothy was not meant strictly for him, because each follower of Christ has the same responsibility, the same mantle: to guard the precious truth of the Word of God, to pass these truths along, teaching our children and other trustworthy people. We are to focus our teaching on the resurrection of God the Son and the faithfulness of God the Father. And, having done all this, remain personally accountable and faithful to God's Word.

"Tell me the stories of Jesus, write on my heart every word; Tell me the stories most precious, sweetest that ever was heard." Frances J. Crosby, pub. 1880.

You are part of the miracle of Living Tradition. Take it seriously, carefully and joyfully as God uses you, along with the Bible and the Holy Spirit, to impart His truth to the next generation. What an honor this is. Thank you, Lord. May we be faithful to the call in all humility for God's glory and the life of the world.

--- *the* B o o k *of* ---

TITUS

what you do

flows from

who you are

Everything is pure

to those whose hearts are pure. But nothing is pure to those who
are corrupt and unbelieving, because their minds and consciences
are corrupted. Titus 1:15 NLT

There had been followers of Christ living on the Island of Crete since just
after Jesus' resurrection. Jewish Cretans would have been attending Passover
in Jerusalem when Jesus was crucified, buried and rose again from the dead.
Most of these would stay in Jerusalem the following weeks through Pentecost.
These Cretan Jews would have been among those who heard the Gospel in
their own language.

(both Jews and converts to Judaism), Cretans, and Arabs. And
we all hear these people speaking in our own languages about the
wonderful things God has done! Acts 2:11 NKJV

These newly baptized believers brought the message of Christ back to the
Island, and pockets of believers began to gather as more people from this
primarily irreligious island heard the Good News about Jesus.

Meanwhile, Titus had met Paul, been baptized and became one of Paul's dear-
est companions. History tells us that Titus was a pious man from his youth,
abstaining from the pleasure-oriented lifestyle of his peers. He was careful
to maintain his virginity which is a meaningful sign that he was disciplined,
counter-cultural and pure of heart.

Paul and Titus visited Crete on one of the late missionary journeys. Paul had
Titus remain there to appoint elders and bring some order to the churches
that God rose up on the island. Other than a brief time when Titus went to
Rome while Paul was awaiting trial, Titus stayed on Crete and became the first
Bishop of Crete. True to Paul's letter, Bishop Titus established Christianity on

the island with a foundation that has survived two thousand years.

The task Titus was given was not just to teach sound doctrine, but also to observe and appoint elders in the churches. Paul wrote about what Titus needed to seek in a person's character to know if he or she would be a good leader. As a man who had a pure heart, Titus was able to discern the motivations of the young Christians by watching and listening to them.

An elder must live a blameless life. He must be faithful to his wife, and his children must be believers who don't have a reputation for being wild or rebellious. A church leader is a manager of God's household, so he must live a blameless life. He must not be arrogant or quick-tempered; he must not be a heavy drinker, violent, or dishonest with money. Rather, he must enjoy having guests in his home, and he must love what is good. He must live wisely and be just. He must live a devout and disciplined life. Titus 1:6-8 NLT

One of the things that people in our generation have always struggled with is this idea of being different inside of our home, with our own family, than we are in the workplace or at church. Many have stories of spouses or parents and children arguing every Sunday morning, struggling to get out the door, only to be the perfect family as soon as they cross the threshold into the church building. Many of us can relate with that scenario and laugh. But, it can create stress, anger, resentment and all kinds of negative feelings that can grow between loved ones like weeds growing up through a crack in the concrete, revealing what is underneath.

Our character and conduct are a product of the condition of our heart. We can't get by in life pretending to be something that we are not. The truth will come out. Jesus said:

Whatever you have said in the dark will be heard in the light, and what you have whispered behind closed doors will be shouted from the housetops for all to hear! Luke 12:3 NLT

When God our Savior revealed his kindness and love, he saved us, not because of the righteous things we had done, but because of his mercy. He washed away our sins, giving us a new birth and new life through the Holy Spirit. He generously poured out the Spirit upon us through Jesus Christ our Savior. Because of his grace he made us right in his sight and gave us confidence that we will inherit eternal life. Titus 3:4-7 NLT

Because of God's grace and mercy, not our self-righteousness or goodness, our hearts can be renewed through His kindness and love. It is not because we're perfect, but because of His generous love.

What we do flows from who we are, and who we are can change and be renewed by the grace of God.

If secret hypocrisy challenges your worthiness to serve, go to the altar at church or kneel by your bedside right now, and repent and pray.

Create in me a clean heart, O God. Renew a loyal spirit within me. Psalm 51:10 NLT

He will—because He loves you so much!

--- *the* B o o k *of* ---

PHILEMON

the generosity

that comes

from faith

And I am praying
that you will put into action the generosity that comes from your faith as you understand and experience all the good things we have in Christ. Philemon 1:6 NLT

What an amazing story! A slave named Onesimus ran away from his home in Colossae and made it to Rome before he was arrested and jailed. His owner had no idea where he'd gone. All he knew was that it was bad for business. A servant earned his way like a field animal or a piece of equipment. One missing meant lost revenue, bad morale among the staff, and an angry owner. This is not to excuse slavery of any kind. It is not right, but keep in mind, this is set in the first century.

We aren't told how everything transpired. We can only imagine the chain of events and conversations that may have taken place: While in prison the young slave met the Apostle Paul. He is saved, changed, made new by Jesus Christ and baptized. Possibly because of his background, he became an assistant to the apostle, helped out and served in any way he could. One day a conversation could have gone something like this:

"So, where are you from, son?" the apostle may have asked.

"Colossae. I was a slave," said Onesimus.

"A slave to man and now a slave of the Lord," the Apostle may have smiled.

"To whom were you a slave?"

"My Master was a man called Philemon."

"Philemon? I know him! He is a good man. And he set you free?" Paul might say.

"I, uh, ran away."

Meanwhile, things were different in Colossae. Philemon and Apphia, his wife, had changed everything from the time before he ran away. Their spacious house had been converted into a house of prayer for the church. Philemon was appointed a leader of the church, a Bishop, while his wife, Apphia, received the sick and vagrants and ministered to their needs. Philemon's and Apphia's lives were completely changed since meeting Jesus Christ, and their testimony of love and generosity became known throughout the region.

"I can't go back. I will stay with you," Onesimus thought.
"No, just the opposite, my son," Paul would decide. "You must go back. Neither you, nor me, nor our brother Philemon should carry this burden through life."

Paul wrote a letter to his friend, Philemon, which asked him to put his generosity into action and receive the young man back, not as a slave, but as a brother. Paul asked; he didn't demand. He told Philemon to charge whatever the young man owes to his own account, and he would repay it.

Philemon did receive the young man back, and they were restored. Then, selflessly, Philemon sent Onesimus back to continue his service to the Apostle Paul.

With that, the spiritual, emotional and even physical chain of bondage over the entire situation was broken, a victory in the heavenly realm. Paul never had to regret employing the young man and keeping the secret from his Christian brother, Philemon. Philemon was released from any seeds of bitterness toward Onesimus and residing anger he felt for being betrayed. And Onesimus was able to apologize, face to face, and repented for his actions toward Philemon and his household. Everyone was released.

Unresolved conflict between people is like a splinter under the skin. Though small and unseen it will prohibit you from full devotion to any task because it demands your attention. There is queasiness in your stomach that never goes away until the issue is resolved. Life is too short to harbor unresolved conflict with others. It is a festering splinter.

Historically, much of this story took place while Nero was emperor of Rome and persecution of Christians was rampant. Not too long after Philemon and Onesimus were restored and the young man was sent back to minister to Paul in Rome, there was a pagan feast in Colossae. Christians gathered at the home of Philemon and Apphia to pray. So enraged were the heathens that the Christians were praying for them, they attacked the prayer meeting, dragging away Philemon, Apphia and Archippus, another Christian brother. Archippus was stabbed repeatedly and died.

Philemon and his wife were buried up to their waists and stoned to death.

Paul himself was ultimately martyred under Nero as well.

The only survivor was Onesimus, the former slave. He became a bishop and served faithfully in various cities and regions. In the year 109, over 40 years after being restored to Philemon, Bishop Onesimus was arrested, under the reign of Emperor Trajan, and beheaded for faithfully maintaining his faith in Christ.

Dear one, are there people in your life who have wronged you? Though possibly separated by miles and even years, a splinter remains? Infecting your soul, refusing to go away, always just a small trigger away from causing you pain? Follow the pattern of the holy Apostle Paul. Deal directly with the matter. Put into action the generosity that comes from your faith and release them. Write off the debt they owe; cover them out of generosity. Because you, too, had a debt you could not pay, and Christ generously covered you.

--- *the Book of* ---

HEBREWS

vagabonds
and
castaways

So also Jesus

suffered and died outside the city gates to make his people holy by means of his own blood. So let us go out to him, outside the camp, and bear the disgrace he bore. For this world is not our permanent home; we are looking forward to a home yet to come. Hebrews 13:12-14 NLT

Most of the original Christians were Jewish. They realized by personal experience and revelation of God that Jesus was the Messiah, the Promised Deliverer. To them, Jesus was everything they had been longing for in life. In Christ, every religious tradition they had ever followed now made sense. All the promises of God were "yes" and "amen" in Jesus, all the traditions they had followed were "Aha!" In Christ, they didn't stop being Jewish; they just became completed as Jews.

Hebrews is like a Christian commentary of the Old Testament for these Jewish believers. Hebrews describes how the symbols and shadows, the commandments and traditions so beautifully developed by God and articulated by Moses, from the High Priest to the Temple, all pointed to Christ Jesus.

The problem was, not all of Israel saw the truth as it was in Jesus. Much of the leadership, the Sanhedrin, did not believe Christ had come. They were angry so many people were following Jesus even after their leaders had conspired with Rome to crucify Him. Still the Christians insisted, declaring, "He is risen! Just as He said!"

These believing Jews, still fully Jewish, many still attending synagogue and living Jewish lives, became unwitting targets of scorn, persecuted and rejected by everything around which their lives had revolved. Many were tempted to forsake Christ and return to their former, Savior-less ways, paradoxically longing for One they knew had already come.

But, Hebrews encourages them to stand firm in their faith. For in Jesus, they have gained more than they lost. While no longer considered citizens of Israel, they became full citizens of Heaven, children of God, adopted into an eternal family, invited into God's place of rest by faith in Jesus Christ.

> So God set another time for entering His rest, and that time is today... Hebrews 4:7a NLT

> So there is a special rest still waiting for the people of God. For all who have entered into God's rest have rested from their labors, just as God did after creating the world. So let us do our best to enter that rest... Hebrews 4:9-11a NLT

We enter in by faith.

> Faith shows the reality of what we hope for; it is the evidence of things we cannot see… Hebrews 11:1 NLT
> And it is impossible to please God without faith. Anyone who wants to come to him must believe that God exists and that he rewards those who sincerely seek him. Hebrews 11:6 NLT

> So then, since we have a great High Priest who has entered heaven, Jesus the Son of God, let us hold firmly to what we believe. This High Priest of ours understands our weaknesses, for he faced all of the same testings we do, yet he did not sin. So let us come boldly to the throne of our gracious God. There we will receive his mercy, and we will find grace to help us when we need it most.
> Hebrews 4:14-16 NLT

He understands our weaknesses, our need for mercy, our need for grace. For we, whether Jew or Gentile, are learning what it is like to be the outcast and vagabond.

Even today, following our Heavenly King is illegal in many countries on earth. People who pledge allegiance only to the risen Lord are viewed as somehow dangerous, countercultural and problematic. Earthly kingdoms are threatened by the non-violent peace of Christ and the simplicity of loving and doing good.

Jesus warned that it would be this way.

> **If they persecuted me, they will persecute you …**
> John 15:20 NKJV

> **In the world you will have tribulation; but be of good cheer, I have overcome the world... John 16:33 NKJV**

So we make the unpopular choice. For many of us, it's really not a choice at all; it is simply the truth. We hold it fast because of love. It is faith directed. I love Jesus, and I couldn't "not believe" if I tried. And why would I try? For He is my very Life and Breath, my Hope and First Love.

If that means I must live outside the camp, sharing in His suffering and shame, then so be it. For it is there I find Jesus, Lord of the vagabond, Savior of the castaway, embracing in love all who come to Him by faith.

JAMES

don't
fool
yourself

But don't just listen

to God's word. You must do what it says. Otherwise, you are only fooling yourselves...

If you claim to be religious but don't control your tongue, you are fooling yourself, and your religion is worthless. Pure and genuine religion in the sight of God the Father means caring for orphans and widows in their distress and refusing to let the world corrupt you. James 1:22, 26-27 NLT

James the Just was a relative of Jesus and the first bishop of Jerusalem. We see him in Acts 15 directing the first council at Jerusalem in determining requirements for non-Jewish believers. James may have written this letter not long after the stoning of Deacon Stephen and the onset of Christian persecution which led to the Christians in Jerusalem being scattered throughout the region (Acts 7-8). This would make James one of the earliest New Testament books.

The core idea of this short letter is the harmony of faith and works in the life of a believer. Our human will, our conversation, conduct, behavior and morality express our faith. God's unmerited favor doesn't negate our personal responsibility; on the contrary, our actions are animated by God's grace.

People generally don't have a problem justifying their own behavior. We tend to think we've got life pretty much figured out and, on the whole, are in better spiritual condition than most others. Following this line of thinking, we believe it is largely other people who are being targeted in books like James. In comparing myself with others, I tend to come out looking pretty good. "Sheesh, that guy is a mess. I hope he is reading this. Preach it, pastor; I hope she's listening!" We justify ourselves and never consider that of all the people in the world, James is actually singling us out and saying,

"Hey, you! Yeah, you! I'm talking to you!"

"But, James, I'm not like this at all."
And James says, "Dear one, you're fooling yourself."

I know this is true of myself. My life has been a journey of three steps forward and two steps back. My selfish flesh trips me up like a pair of shoes four sizes too big. My self-perception is that I have the holiest of attributes when, in reality, I can be judgmental, condescending, self-righteous and filled to the brim with false piety.

James wrote his letter to folks like me. Stop fooling yourself. By faith, I exchanged an old life for a new one. If faith can save my soul, can it also help me deny myself? Because that's the core problem.

So James started with three or four disciplines to encourage dependence on the work of the Holy Spirit in our lives, cleaning the crud and correcting our conduct.

> But don't just listen to God's word. You must do what it says. Otherwise, you are only fooling yourselves. James 1:22 NLT

1. Be a doer of the Word, not just a hearer. The verse isn't targeting everyone but me. It's targeting *only* me. Forgive. Humble yourself. Don't judge...

> ...the tongue is a flame of fire. It is a whole world of wickedness, corrupting your entire body. It can set your whole life on fire, for it is set on fire by hell itself. James 3:6 NLT

2. Control your tongue. Don't be a hypocrite. Don't demean, curse or self-deprecate. Instead, build up, bless, honor, use words for good and never harm.

> Pure and genuine religion in the sight of God the Father means caring for orphans and widows in their distress and refusing to let

the world corrupt you. James 1:27 NLT

3. Take care of the needy, the infirm, hurting, orphan and widow. Helping people shouldn't be a ministry or an outlet, it should be our lifestyle. James calls it pure and undefiled religion because it is wholly "others focused." There is no room for the impurity of selfish gain.

4. Refuse to let the world corrupt you. We really want this one to point to everyone else because we think we can handle the world and we're wise to its ways. "Coarse language may bother others, but not me. Others shouldn't watch immoral video content, but it doesn't affect me. Others can't deal with social media addiction, but I keep it balanced." Or any of a million other ways the world will sneak into a crack in your armor and corrupt you. Satan is a deceiver, a liar. That's not just what he does, *it's who he is.* He will try everything to corrupt you and weaken your witness of God's truth. Resist the devil, and he will flee from you.

Dear one, as we regularly deal with our own foolishness through repentance, fasting and prayer, we will be more able to help others from a pure heart and selfless intentions. This is Jesus' way. Then, when we see a brother wandering into madness and folly, we can help him find his way back to the simplicity of Christ.

If these words ring true in your heart, pray this simple prayer of repentance before the Lord saying something like this: "Lord Jesus forgive me. Help me see myself as I really am. I want to stop fooling myself. I want to live in honesty and truth, transparent before You and my loved ones. In Jesus' Name, Amen."

--- *the* B o o k *of* ---

I PETER

the key to
enduring
suffering

All praise to God,

the Father of our Lord Jesus Christ. It is by his great mercy that we have been born again, because God raised Jesus Christ from the dead. Now we live with great expectation,

1 Peter 1:3 NLT

Who would have thought that the rugged commercial fisherman, the "man's man" of the disciples, would live to become a great encourager of other believers? This first letter, 1 Peter, is about dealing with suffering, written with comfort and great encouragement contained in each of the five chapters.

Unjust suffering will likely be a part of the Christian life—pain, persecution, misunderstanding, offense, disease and more. This was certainly true in Peter's day, when Emperor Nero was on a warpath against believers, and as evident by Peter's own death by way of crucifixion (upside down).

Woven subtly through the letter, though, is a beautiful key to enduring suffering. Peter knew it. He'd been preaching it since the (first) Pentecost. It isn't a secret or a revelation or a play on words. It is a present reality through which we can endure any hardship.

Live out of your baptism. Baptism is sacramental. A sacrament is when God infuses with His presence, something relatively ordinary, in this case, a pool of water, thus, making it holy and something that, outside of that context, it could not otherwise be. In the case of baptism, the water becomes both a tomb and a womb; a tomb where the old man dies, and a womb where new life is birthed.

Remember in Romans, the Apostle Paul wrote:

> Or do you not know that as many of us as were baptized into Christ Jesus were baptized into His death? Therefore we were buried with

Him through baptism into death, that just as Christ was raised
from the dead by the glory of the Father, even so we also should
walk in newness of life. Romans 6:3-4 NKLV

When we are raised from the water of holy baptism, we are born again, "**born
of water and of spirit**" as Jesus told Nicodemus. John 3:5 NKJV

Christ suffered for our sins once for all time. He never sinned, but
he died for sinners to bring you safely home to God. He suffered
physical death, but he was raised to life in the Spirit...
1 Peter 3:18 NLT

...And that water (flood of Noah) is a picture of baptism, which
now saves you, not by removing dirt from your body, but as a
response to God from a clean conscience. It is effective because of
the resurrection of Jesus Christ. 1 Peter 3:20-21 NLT

After you are baptized, the raw material of your body, the water, bone and
blood, may be the same, but your life and very essence is different. Your soul is
alive to God, your spirit animated with His own. Now you have a Guardian for
your soul, and your new life is hidden with Christ in God.

You can now live out of the reality of what actually happened; you were made
new! The trials and tribulations of life will no longer take the toll on you that
they once did. You are forgiven, free, chosen, brand new! You can rest in your
new life in the resurrected Lord Jesus Christ!

Since you have been raised to new life with Christ, set your sights
on the realities of heaven, where Christ sits in the place of honor at
God's right hand. Think about the things of heaven, not the things
of earth. For you died to this life, and your real life is hidden with
Christ in God. Colossians 3:1-3 NLT

Living out of this reality will empower you to endure anything.

I am a new creation in Christ, In His death, I died,
In His resurrection, I was raised—Now by His grace, I stand.

2 PETER

the light
of God's
patience

And remember,

our Lord's patience gives people time to be saved.

2 Peter 3:15 NLT

There comes a point in a person's life when they realize they aren't going to live forever. The Bible reminds us that, **"It is appointed unto a man once to die and then the judgment..."** Hebrews 9:27. You know it in a broad sense when you are young, but it doesn't usually hit home until your later years when it dawns on you that life is short—fleeting.

Peter was dealing with this when he sat down to write his second letter. Along with the other apostles, he had faithfully led the fledgling church since God, the Holy Spirit, had filled them all, empowering them to preach the truths about Jesus Christ and make disciples of all nations. Now thirty-something years later, with the Gospel of Jesus Christ changing lives across the known world, growing and expanding, the Lord nudged Peter's heart and told him it was about time to hang up his sandals.

> **For our Lord Jesus Christ has shown me that I must soon leave this earthly life, so I will work hard to make sure you always remember these things after I am gone. 2 Peter 1:14-15 NLT**

He probably didn't realize it at that moment, but Nero would soon have him executed, crucified upside down, as the evil emperor sought to terrorize and crush the peaceable movement of Christ.

What do you say when you get to say one last thing? What do you want to leave people to remember?

As he looked at the young church, Peter, by inspiration of the Holy Spirit, decided to write about some current issues, specifically, the Kingdom of God, false teaching and the second coming of Jesus Christ.

His short letter applies as much today as the day it was written, and it can be distilled down to this:

How should we live our lives in the context of the patience of God?

Even then, in the middle of the first century, Christians were anticipating the second coming of Christ. Life was hard, and persecution was rampant. Pressure from the religious establishment was nonstop. So they held fast to Jesus' promise, thinking, "surely Christ will return and deliver us from all this..."

How many of us have looked heavenward and cried out for the same thing? "Come, Lord Jesus, deliver us, set this place right!" And, yet He has not returned.

The false teachers and religious people seized upon Jesus' apparent negligence, trying to mislead the believers like the serpent in the garden of Eden, *"Did God say?..."*

So, Peter reminds us that God exists outside of the realm of time that He created. Time is something He created for us, not for Himself. Where we see days turning into months and years, God doesn't. God isn't bound this way.

A day is like a thousand years to the Lord, and a thousand years is like a day. 2 Peter 3:8 NLT

His promised return is certain. That's the important thing.

Two thousand years later, there are so many belief systems and theories and "isms" about the Second Coming of Jesus that there are cottage industries supporting proponents of one view or another. But, Peter didn't speculate. He made it plain and clear.

The Lord isn't really being slow about his promise, as some people

think. No, he is being patient for your sake. He does not want anyone to be destroyed, but wants everyone to repent.

2 Peter 3:9 NLT

By His boundless, timeless, unfailing love, God has been waiting for you to
give Him your heart. He is waiting for people in Nepal and Somalia and the
remotest Islands of Indonesia to hear the Good News about Jesus and turn
to Him, and other people we don't know, from every nation tribe and tongue.
We don't know them, but He surely does. Then He will come back—on His
terms, not ours.

How then should we live in light of this kind of patience?

First, we should live godly lives and God has given us everything we need.

By his divine power, God has given us everything we need for
living a godly life. We have received all of this by coming to know
him, the one who called us to himself by means of his marvelous
glory and excellence. 2 Peter 1:3 NLT

Then, don't rest on yesterday's faith but continue to pursue a more and more
virtuous life.

Supplement your faith with a generous provision of moral excellence, and moral excellence with knowledge, and knowledge with
self-control, and self-control with patient endurance, and patient
endurance with godliness, and godliness with brotherly affection,
and brotherly affection with love for everyone. The more you grow
like this, the more productive and useful you will be in your knowledge of our Lord Jesus Christ. 2 Peter 1:5-8 NLT

Don't stop living in anticipation of the Lord's return. He will come again some day as He said. Until then, keep living, keep growing in love, grace, faith and humility. Live simple, peaceable, virtuous lives that manifest the difference between walking with Jesus and following the hectic and selfish ways of a broken world.

I JOHN

risk love - this is real

We proclaim to you

the one who existed from the beginning, whom we have heard and seen. We saw him with our own eyes and touched him with our own hands. He is the Word of life. This one who is life itself was revealed to us, and we have seen him. And now we testify and proclaim to you that he is the one who is eternal life. He was with the Father, and then he was revealed to us.

1 John 1:1-2 NLT

It was the end of the first century. John, called to follow Jesus while a young man, possibly a teenager, was now an old man. He was likely the last remaining apostle and possibly the last remaining eyewitness of Jesus Christ, the Son of God.

John wrote largely to people who trusted Christ Jesus based on the testimony of someone else. These were second and third generation Christians, those who believed because their parents told them about the cross and the resurrection, or they had heard the Apostle Paul and were convicted by his single-minded passion, and they believed.

But no matter how they heard, almost all of them were like you and me. They believed in Jesus even though they had never seen Him.

John, the disciple Jesus loved, the disciple who leaned on Jesus at the Last Supper as a child might rest against the safety of a parent (John 21:20), wrote a letter to those of us who weren't there.

It is the simplest of messages: Jesus is real, the stories are true, you can risk love, you

won't be hurt, dear one, you will be healed.

God became a man. People saw Him, touched Him, talked with Him. He was with the Father from the beginning and now has been revealed to us. He is eternal life. You can know Him with the same intimacy as the very disciples.

> We proclaim to you what we ourselves have actually seen and heard so that you may have fellowship with us. And our fellowship is with the Father and with his Son, Jesus Christ. 1 John 1:3 NLT

Jesus was a real man, flesh and blood just like you and me. And, He was the Son of God, literally God in the flesh, simultaneously God and man. His life demonstrated to the world what real humanity and real love look like. Jesus is the perfect example of what it means to be human.

> We know what real love is because Jesus gave up his life for us. So we also ought to give up our lives for our brothers and sisters... Dear children, let's not merely say that we love each other; let us show the truth by our actions. 1 John 3:16,18 NLT

Loving to this extent, laying down one's life, isn't a normal trait in a fallen world. Self preservation is. People tend to save themselves first, then help others if possible. Taking the risk to love others the way Jesus did shows that God the Holy Spirit is living in us, and He is truly changing our hearts because people don't naturally love with such selfless love.

> We must believe in the name of his Son, Jesus Christ, and love one another, just as he commanded us. Those who obey God's commandments remain in fellowship with him, and he with them. And we know he lives in us because the Spirit he gave us lives in us.
> 1 John 3:23-24 NLT

John and the other disciples didn't just have fellowship with Jesus before the crucifixion and for a brief few weeks after His resurrection. John is saying that His fellowship with Christ has continued throughout his life, as God embraces people with the love of Christ through his simple life. And it will be the same for us.

> God showed how much he loved us by sending his one and only Son into the world so that we might have eternal life through him. This is real love—not that we loved God, but that he loved us and sent his Son as a sacrifice to take away our sins. Dear friends, since God loved us that much, we surely ought to love each other. No one has ever seen God. But if we love each other, God lives in us, and his love is brought to full expression in us. And God has given us his Spirit as proof that we live in him and he in us.
> 1 John 4:9-13 NLT

Jesus is real. His love is real. Forgiveness is real. Risk loving others, it is how God lives in us and how His love is revealed to others.

> We love each other because He loved us first. 1 John 4:19 NLT

This is how we share in the kingdom, how we share fellowship with the apostles and saints, with Christ Himself, by being a selfless vessel through whom the Living Christ can continue to love people and draw them to forgiveness, healing and wholeness.

2 JOHN

the doctrine
of
Christ

Whoever

transgresses and does not abide in the doctrine of Christ does not have God. He who abides in the doctrine of Christ has both the Father and the Son. 2 John 1:9 NKJV

The Apostle John refers to the church to whom he is writing as "the elect lady and her children." (v1 NKJV). Then closing the letter, John concludes, "the children of your elect sister greet you." (v13 NKJV). Have you ever referred to your church as an "elect lady?" You may have heard the term "sister" churches, and this is where that idea originated. What a beautiful expression of the local church as the bride of Christ, "the elect lady."

In this brief letter written near the end of the first century, John simply reiterates two priorities of the "elect lady," the local church and why they are critical.

1. Love one another

I am writing to remind you, dear friends, that we should love one another. This is not a new commandment, but one we have had from the beginning. Love means doing what God has commanded us, and he has commanded us to love one another, just as you heard from the beginning. 2 John 1:5-6 NLT

2. Abide in the doctrine of Christ

For many deceivers have gone out into the world who do not confess Jesus Christ as coming in the flesh. This is a deceiver and an antichrist... 2 John 1:7 NKJV

Whoever transgresses and does not abide in the doctrine of Christ does not have God. He who abides in the doctrine of Christ has both the Father and the Son... 2 John 1:9 NKJV

These two, loving one another and abiding in the doctrine of Christ, are the purposes John wants to be the focus of the church.

In his first letter, John wrote:

> **Beloved, let us love one another. For love is of God and everyone who loves is born of God and knows God. He who does not love does not know God for God is love. 1 John 4:7-8 NKJV**

Truly being able to express the love of God to one another in meaningful, redemptive ways, requires knowing Him, abiding in Him. For this, we must understand the doctrine of Christ.

John pointed out those who **"do not confess Jesus Christ as coming in the flesh."** (2 John 1:7) And thus revealed the essence of the doctrine of Christ: that Jesus Christ, the Son of God, was fully human and fully God. Jesus was/is God incarnate, in flesh.

So important and yet so easily misunderstood, this is the key to understanding everything else about Christianity.

Early in church history, all the bishops gathered over several sessions (councils) and hashed out a Statement of Faith, now called The Nicene Creed, which presents the key points of accepted Christian doctrine in one memorable document.

The most detailed part of the Creed is the second part which explains the doctrine of Christ. As the Apostle John had warned, deceivers had gone into the world seeking to customize the Christian faith into one that fit their personal taste or bias. So the bishops systematically address each of these heresies.

The second part of the Creed reads:

"And (we believe) in one Lord Jesus Christ, the Son of God, the only-begotten, begotten of the Father before all ages. Light of Light; true God of true God; begotten, not made; of one essence with the Father, by whom all things were made; who for us men and for our salvation came down from heaven, and was incarnate of the Holy Spirit and the Virgin Mary, and became man. And He was crucified for us under Pontius Pilate, and suffered, and was buried. And the third day He rose again, according to the Scriptures; and ascended into heaven, and sits at the right hand of the Father; and He shall come again with glory to judge the living and the dead; whose Kingdom shall have no end."

There is more to the Creed that is essential to our faith as Christians, but this is the doctrine of Christ, each of the points taken from passages of Scripture in order to refute bad doctrine.

Paul told Timothy:

Take heed to yourself and to the doctrine. Continue in them, for in doing this you will save both yourself and those who hear you.
1 Timothy 4:16

What you believe is important:

He who abides in the doctrine of Christ has both the Father and the Son. 2 John 1:9 NKJV

--- *the* Book *of* ---

3 JOHN

beloved

Gaius

To the beloved

Gaius, whom I love in truth. 3 John 1:1 NKJV

There is a lot in this brief letter to catch a person's attention. Some preachers never get past the first verse where the words "prosper" and "health" catch their imagination and become proof-texts for all manner of out-of-context theologizing.

Others focus on leadership, the good kind, in the letter modeled by Gaius, and the bad, demonstrated selfishly by Diotrephes who, **"loves to have preeminence... prating against us with malicious words." 3 John 1:9,10 NKJV**

For others, the greeting itself brings pause. The great Apostle John was known as the "beloved disciple," or "the disciple Jesus loved," (John 20:2 NKJV) and here he addresses his brief letter to Gaius, and refers to him as "beloved." It seems that the love that John felt from Jesus, was for his dear friend, Gaius.

I love you like Jesus loves me.

If you are a follower of Christ, you probably carry a deep sense of His love for you.

But, if someone asked you what His love feels like, it might be difficult to articulate in human terms. Because His love is a Divine love, expressed through the sacrificial humanity of Christ, the God-man. It is a bigger love than we can naturally give, although it is wonderful and indescribable to receive.

Solomon may have come close to articulating Divine love when he gazed at his beloved and said, **"You are perfect, there is no flaw in you."** (Song of Solomon 4:7). I think that's how perfect love views the object of their affection, with boundless grace that covers every imperfection like a robe of righteousness. This is how God loves everyone who walks in the truth. This is the kind of love that draws us to holiness.

How was John able to feel that for another person? To say people are not perfect would be a vast understatement. If you're looking, you can probably find some pretty big flaws in just about anyone. I think John could love like Jesus because the old apostle was beginning to partake of the divine nature Peter wrote about, and he just didn't see the flaws anymore; he saw the image of God in people—beauty.

As Christians, we are not supposed to remain the same. Our love and godly attributes are to grow as we are conformed more into the image of Christ and are transformed by the renewing of our minds. We won't reach a perfect state in this flesh-bound body, but that is the direction we are to be heading nevertheless, to Christ-likeness. And, someday, God willing, as we grow in Christ, we will begin to see things more as Jesus sees them, feel things the way Jesus feels them. And, love people the way the Son of God loves them.

So, while I certainly loved my wife on our wedding day, neither of us would have said that I loved her as deeply as Jesus did. She was my love, but she was His beloved— perfect, with no flaw. I loved her with my whole heart, but my heart was still more flesh than spirit, more selfish than divine.

But, through the miracle of God's holy sacrament our love has grown. As we have gotten closer to Jesus, we have grown closer to each other. As we become more Christ-like, we begin to see each other more like Jesus has always seen us—perfect, clothed in His own righteousness, the apple of His eye.

While we are still twenty or thirty years younger now than the apostle John was when he wrote this letter, we are well along the same journey that he had almost completed. John could see people who walked in the truth the same way Jesus saw them.

We're not there yet, but we're not where we used to be. We are inching forward. When I read something as simple as "to the beloved Gaius," I think of God's love for me and long to love all those around me with that same Divine love.

JUDE

God is

able

...keep yourselves
in the love of God. Jude 1:21a NKJV

Jude intended to write about our common faith, but false teachers had crept in unnoticed and began pushing, pulling and redirecting the church in evil ways that reflected their own bias and selfishness. He needed to address this falsehood head-on.

Jude was livid. He didn't mince words in calling out the false teachers

(They are) **clouds without water, trees without fruit, twice dead, pulled up by the roots; and raging waves of the sea, foaming up their own shame, and wandering stars for whom is reserved the blackness of darkness forever."**
Jude 1:12-13 NKJV

False teaching is a scourge on the church. Human nature is such that selfish people are always angling for a way to turn a buck. Sadly, religion provides a pretty good cover for "wandering stars." But, Jude reassures the church that the presence of false teachers is no surprise to the apostles. They had regularly encouraged the believers to be on the lookout for these squirrels with nutty doctrine.

He encouraged us to **"keep yourselves in the love of God..."**(v21), which, on the surface, sounds easy enough. But, then I think about myself and my best intentions and realize I can hardly keep myself on an eating or exercise schedule, how could I ever hope to keep myself in the love of God? I think Jude knows this about human nature, so he shares some pointers as to how we can accomplish this:

1. Build yourself up on your most holy faith. Jude 1:20 NKJV

In part, this means filling your life with more of God's Holy Word as **"faith comes by hearing and hearing by the word of God."** (Romans 10:17 NKJV). To the extent that our hearts and minds are filled with God's word, the confident assurance of the gospel will reside in the front of our minds, bringing a ready supply of courage and faith right when we need it.

2. Praying in the Holy Spirit." Jude 1:20 NKJV

Paul wrote that when we don't know how to pray as we ought to that the Holy Spirit intercedes for us with groaning and uttering that we don't necessarily comprehend. (Romans 8:26 NLT). Praying in the Holy Spirit is a deep and beautiful prayer of surrender that may begin with, "Oh God, help me..." and, after a deep breath or two, and a sigh, we hand the reigns over to "Christ in us," the Holy Spirit, to express a depth of need we know we have but can't seem to articulate.

3. Look for the mercy of our Lord Jesus Christ unto eternal life. Jude 1:21b NKJV

This involves the confidence of Christ's return and eternal life with Him. Salvation is certainly the assurance of eternal life with Christ, but it is, at the same time, wholeness, forgiveness, healing and life with Christ now, during our life on earth. Watching expectantly for the return of Christ helps keep us in the love of God because His mercy today brings the assurance of eternity tomorrow.

4. And on some have compassion... but others save with fear... Jude 1:22-23 NKJV

Stay outwardly focused. One way to remain in the love of God is to take our eyes off ourselves. That's the paradox of faith. If I desire to live, I must die to myself. Serving others as an ambassador of Christ is why God has placed us in the world at this time. If you were born to earth just to be saved, God would have taken you to heaven the moment you confessed faith in Christ. But, He usually doesn't do it that way. Generally, He leaves us here for the sake of someone else. Focusing on others is a way God anoints you to remain in His love.

So keep yourself in the love of God, and, in so doing, protect yourselves and your churches from the curse of false teaching. Think you might fall short? Don't worry, Jesus will always have your back. For **"(He) is able to keep you from stumbling, And to present you faultless Before the presence of His glory..." Jude 1:24 NKJV**

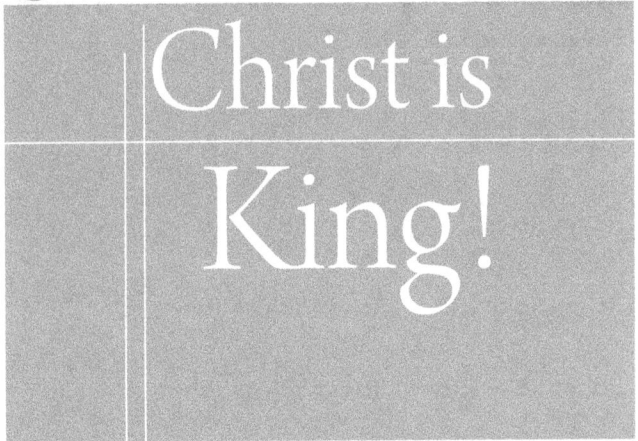

--- *the Book of* ---

REVELATION

Christ is King!

Now I saw heaven

opened, and behold, a white horse. And He who sat on him was called Faithful and True, and in righteousness He judges and makes war. His eyes were like a flame of fire, and on His head were many crowns. He had a name written that no one knew except Himself. He was clothed with a robe dipped in blood, and His name is called The Word of God. And the armies in heaven, clothed in fine linen, white and clean, followed Him on white horses. Now out of His mouth goes a sharp sword, that with it He should strike the nations. And He Himself will rule them with a rod of iron. He Himself treads the winepress of the fierceness and wrath of Almighty God. And He has on His robe and on His thigh a name written: KING OF KINGS AND LORD OF LORDS. Revelation 19:11-16

"Now I saw heaven opened, and behold..." In the book of Revelation, God gave a vision of the end times to the old apostle John, when he was probably in his nineties and in exile for his faith, on the remote island of Patmos. John chronicled what he was shown and called the vision, the "Apocalypse," or the "Revelation," which means revealing, unveiling, or taking the cover off something. In this case, the return of Jesus Christ is revealed.

The end of the first century was a dangerous time for Christians in the Roman Empire. Beginning with Nero, the rulers of Rome had become more and more determined to rid the empire of Christ's followers. Domitian, possibly the most bloodthirsty emperor, was making life miserable for Christians around the time John was writing the Revelation.

About twenty years earlier, Emperor Titus had destroyed the temple in
Jerusalem. This was something Jesus said would happen. In Matthew 24, Jesus
mentions the temple destruction just before talking about the tribulation that
would occur before His second coming. Those who had heard these words
from the apostles teaching would have doubtlessly connected the dots and
believed Christ's return was now imminent, that He would be coming any
moment.

Some would be energized by the possibility, and others would be burdened,
unsure if they could make it through all the tribulation coming against them
at every side. So our loving, omniscient God unveils the future for the church,
the final victory of Christ and His eternal kingdom.

The Revelation includes at least three complimentary themes:

First, to the churches and Christians who are living through grievous tribulation: hold fast, persevere, overcome the obstacles and stand firm in the faith,
for it will all be worth it in the end.

Second, it is also a book of prophecy that speaks in detail of a time to come in
the future, the physical return of Jesus Christ.

And third, Revelation describes, allegorically, the ongoing conflict between
God and Satan, good and evil, and the free-thinking people of God's kingdom
and unwitting pawns of the devil.

We shouldn't be afraid to read Revelation. In fact, God promises a blessing for
those who read and observe the book.

> Blessed is he who reads and those who hear the words of this
> prophecy, and keep those things which are written in it; for the
> time is near. Revelation 1:3 NKJV

When reading Revelation, it is best not to get too caught up in interpreting what John meant in the language he used, equating his vision with modern technology or figuring out various timelines and theories. Instead, just let the Lord minister assurance and love to you as He confirms that everything is going according to plan, God is in charge. The King is coming!

He who testifies to these things says, "Surely I am coming quickly."

Amen. Even so, come, Lord Jesus!

The grace of our Lord Jesus Christ be with you all. Amen.

Revelation 22:20-21 NKJV

325
BOOKS
Our Life in Christ

THE LITTLE BOOK OF VIRTUES
14 ways your life can reflect the beauty of God.

www.ingramcontent.com/pod-product-compliance
Lightning Source LLC
LaVergne TN
LVHW051254080426
835509LV00020B/2966